The Cameo Series
Number 1

Jo

(185    )31)

By Jeff Smallcombe

The Cameo Series
Number 1


**Joseph** is the biographical account of the
life and times of an illegitimate Gloucestershire
workhouse boy, born in 1850, who became a
Cardiff entrepreneur, and died in 1931.


This privately published book
is limited to one hundred copies
This copy is number 37 /100

Copyright Dr. J. Smallcombe 2002
Published by Dr. J. Smallcombe
Printed by Parchment (Oxford) Ltd
ISBN  0-9542194-0-6

# Table of Contents

# Illustrations

# Illustrations (continued)

# ENTREATY

The diagrams, illustrations and pictures in this book are not there to fill space; they are placed strategically to enhance the story of Joseph, to help the reader to assimilate the ambience of the time. I entreat the reader to look at the picture of the workhouse and imagine what went on behind its stark walls. Look at the crinoline dress, and imagine having to negotiate delicate household objects. Look at St. Jude's Church and imagine the wedding of the illegitimate ostler and the servant girl, probably dressed up for the first time in their lives. Look at the hansom cab and imagine its driver sitting in the open urging the horses on a bitter January night with driving rain and sleet. Every picture should be worth a thousand words; please let them play their part.

The front and back covers are taken from John Washbourne's photographs, of John Hollister's original pictures of Joseph and Harriet Smallcombe.

# Acknowledgements

I would like to thank Vicky Tucker for her assistance in the research into the part of the story found in Yate. I would also like to thank Patricia Alcock for her 'Whispers from the Workhouse', which in the early days of my research into the Chipping Sodbury Union Workhouse was inspirational.

The bulk of Joseph's life was spent in Cardiff, and I acknowledge the dedicated research of Madeleine Rawlings, in uncovering text, maps, pictures, and even bottles that fleshed out the bones of Joseph's story.

No work of this nature is possible without the assistance of the Register Offices, Records Offices and Libraries, particularly those at Bristol, Yate and Cardiff, whose knowledgeable staff are so helpful and co-operative. I would like to thank Colin Jones, John Andrews and Mr. Brynmor Jones of Cardiff Central Library, Local Studies, and for permission to reproduce their photographs of Cardiff, and in particularly Stewart Williams for his assistance and permission to reproduce photographs from his "Cardiff Yesterday" series.

I must also acknowledge the contribution of the 'Museum of Bath at Work' to the section on Joseph's manufacturing activities. The magnificent display of a complete mineral water manufacturing plant, and the assistance with copies of contemporary literature from trade magazines of the time was invaluable. All the illustrations in that Chapter are reproduced by the kind permission of the Museum.

I am grateful to The Bath & North East Somerset Heritage Services for providing the illustrations of the costumes in Chapters One and Four.

In the latter stages my contact with Joseph's great grandchildren provided a valuable insight into many aspects of Joseph's family. I should particularly like to mention John Hollister of Yate, descended from Beatrice, and Rita Davis of Cardiff, descended from Harriet Hannah, for anecdotes from their respective ends of the family, and Rita for numerous family pictures and several trips to Cardiff Library for me. John Washbourne provided copies of the pictures of Joseph and Harriet owned by John Hollister, and Bob Janes, related to the Dyer family, provided the story of the Wickwar Gang,

I would like to thank Mr. Squires for showing me the inside of 38 Clare Road, for allowing me to see the yard and buildings behind 12 and 14 Allerton Street, and also for the sight of Joseph's original deeds and mortgage documents for those premises.

Finally I would like to thank Bill Barrett, the well-known local Cardiff historian for perusing the manuscript for me, in spite of his efforts I still lay claim to all the errors and omission I managed to squeeze past him.

**Other publications by the same author.**

A Thumbnail Sketch of The English Legal System
A Thumbnail Sketch of Employment Law
A Thumbnail Sketch of Industrial Tribunals
A Thumbnail Sketch of Contact Law
A Thumbnail Sketch of Tort
A Thumbnail Sketch of Oral Communication Skills

# Introduction

This might not be the most spectacular story ever told, it may not be the most heart rendering, but it is the story of an unfortunate child given the worst possible start in life, save his health and intellect, who pulled himself from the mire by his bootlaces. This boy, Joseph Smallcombe, started life not just with nothing, but with a severe mark against his name, being an illegitimate workhouse boy. Joseph's mother, Hannah, had eight illegitimate children, six of them in the workhouse at Yate, and twins in a rooming house in Scarborough, but that is another story. Joseph was the eldest of Hannah's Smallcombe's children, and there is no way of knowing whether or not he had any contact with her after he grew up and married. Indeed it is not even possible to be sure whether or not he had much contact with her after his baptism.

There are, however, some very peculiar features about the family record. Hannah's twins, Harry and Eliza, were born in Scarborough on the 14th of March 1875. Harry married in Brighton on the 3rd November 1900, and in 1914 he and his family lived at 20 Westview Terrace, Steelworks, Ebbw Vale. Hannah's first child Joseph was born in 1850, and Harry, his brother, was born in 1875. This is a twenty-five year age difference that leads to two peculiar coincidences. Firstly, with no signs of contact, these two brothers, born twenty-five years and two hundred and fifty miles apart, were both living in South Wales in 1914, one in Cardiff, and the other in Ebbw Vale, a mere twenty-five miles between them. Even so, there is no evidence that they even knew each other, or were aware of their proximity, but that is not all. The steel works at Ebbw Vale was the home some sixty years earlier of the family of a totally different Hannah Smallcombe, and there were still Smallcombes living in the area in 1914, but again there is no evidence that either family knew of the existence of the other. Perhaps even more remarkable is the fact that Joseph's nephew, Harry's son, Harry David Thomas Smallcombe, married into a Dyer family, as did his uncle Joseph fifty-five years earlier.

I refer to Joseph as a 'Cardiff Entrepreneur', but this should be taken in the dictionary sense as 'one who undertakes a business or enterprise', and nothing more grand. There is no evidence that Joseph was in business other than in a small way; nevertheless, this in itself says something about the man, given his background. It is probable that his background was instrumental in his success, in as much as he might have been more 'moneywise' than many, having had so little at the outset of his life. Class status was significant in Victorian times and it was difficult to move from one social class to another. Although there was not always a definitive line, one instinctively knew to which class one belonged, working, middle or upper, but there were strata even within the classes, upper and lower middle class for example. The pauper, like the 'untouchable' in India was classless. The working class roughly comprised skilled and unskilled workers, labourers, dockers, mariners, railwaymen, engineering workers, and the various grades of foremen and supervisors. The middle class comprised master mariners, office staff, builders, merchants and other tradesmen, and the professions. Joseph was a pauper, who became a working class labourer, moving to management, and then to a tradesman status, described in his will as a 'Gentleman'; in other words he elevated himself through several social classes. Joseph's elevation, however, should not be taken as something unique as there are several stories of rags to riches in the annals of Cardiff history. For example, a Cardiff street vendor became an exceedingly wealthy owner in property, transport and mining on a national scale.

Joseph and I are related to a common 18th century ancestor, but I feel a closer kinship, probably because of similar entrepreneurial parts of our lives. I did not suffer the depravations of Joseph's early life, but nevertheless I feel that I understand him. It was his mother Hannah who first caught my eye, but Joseph's story crystallized long before I could finish the research on Hannah. The story of Joseph developed more easily, due to the fact that my simple story about Hannah Smallcombe has turned out to be the complex story of three Hannah Smallcombes, all born in the same area within a year or two of each other. Unfortunately the Smallcombe name has died out in Joseph's line, but perhaps it will now live on a little longer.

# Chapter One

## Joseph in Gloucestershire
## 1850 - 1872

Joseph was born on Friday the 1st November 1850 to Hannah Smallcombe in the Chipping Sodbury Union Workhouse, which was known locally as the "Spike" because of the prominent spire on it's clock tower. His birth certificate shows no father, but the illiterate Hannah registered his birth by making her mark on Friday the 15th November 1850, before W. B. Limbrick the Registrar, and gave her address as the Union House, Yate. The Baptismal records for St. Mary's, Yate, show that Joseph was baptised on Wednesday the 12th February 1851, and this would almost certainly have been a ceremony at the workhouse, by the vicar or curate of St. Mary's, with Hannah present. It is possible that for these three months Hannah and Joseph were together in the workhouse with the nursing Hannah working in the kitchen, or sewing or laundering.

The next record we have of Joseph and his mother is in the 1851 Census, taken on the night of March 30th and 31st, by which time Joseph would have been 5 months old. It is reasonable to assume that Hannah, as an able bodied woman, had probably been sent out to work from the workhouse by this time, whilst retaining her residence there at night, but she probably saw little of Joseph after their initial time together up to his baptism. Her wages would have been paid to the workhouse authorities in exchange for the keep of herself and that of her child, Joseph. There was no dedicated nursery at the Spike at that time, so it is probable that Joseph was kept in the children's ward where the very young children, and the older children who were not old enough to go out to work, were cared for by designated inmates. It is certain that the information provided at the 1851 Census was not given by Hannah, but came from a central register, because Joseph was not named, but recorded as "Infant Smallcom", although he had already been baptised. He was stated to be one month old, whereas he was five months old, clearly a fact that would not have escaped his mother. This also indicates that, in general, the workhouse records might leave something to be desired.

It is difficult to comprehend the conditions and atmosphere of the early Victorian workhouse from our more enlightened stand-point, but it is not beyond our modern experience to realise that what is right or desirable is not always translated into actions at ground level. The practical day-to-day law on the workhouse floor was not always that intended by the legislature, and although matters were corrected from time to time by the censure of officers responsible for any misdemeanours, this was no comfort to those suffering from the day-to-day whims of those in immediate authority. The stories of the hard life lived in these establishments are substantiated in part by reports of people starving to death, rather than go into the workhouse during this period.

The entrance to the Chipping Sodbury Union Workhouse
at Station Road, Yate.

In all probability Joseph had at least as good medical care in the workhouse nursery as he would have done in the arms of his illiterate pauper mother outside of the workhouse. The workhouse records indicate that in 1853 Joseph would have received a vaccination against cholera, which at that time was prevalent in Gloucestershire, and which was still in Sodbury in 1854, due to defective drains. It is unlikely that Hannah could have afforded the half crown to have this done outside of the workhouse or, even if she could have afforded it, whether she would have bothered.

It is impossible to know exactly what was the relationship between Joseph and his mother at any time, and there is no record of Joseph between the 1851 and the 1861 Censuses. It is probable that they led independent lives, perhaps seeing each other in passing, with Joseph initially occupied as a working infant within the workhouse. From the age of four or five Joseph would have been able to assist in the nursery, and then later be engaged in menial tasks around the workhouse, whilst getting a basic education at the Union School. In this he would have the advantage of his mother who was unable to read or write.

It is worth a moment's reflection at this point to consider Joseph's position. These are the formative years for any young child. To be born either illegitimately, or to be born in a workhouse, created a permanent social stigma even in early Victorian times. To be born illegitimately, and in a workhouse doubles the handicap. Not only did Joseph not know the protection of a father, or the companionship of a family, he was also deprived of the comfort of a mother in his everyday life. Workhouse children had little protection as there were no children's protection societies, and the children had no family to turn to for assistance and guidance. Joseph probably felt alone and vulnerable in his early years, but the question it raises is how it formed his character for the rest of his life.

In all probability Joseph was sent out to work at about seven years of age, and the 1861 Census, held on Sunday-Monday 7th - 8th April, shows Joseph "Smallcom" as a farm servant at the age of ten. He is recorded on the Census return for the workhouse, which indicates that he was resident there and working as an outworker, returning to the workhouse at night, and probably working quite close to the workhouse. The Census also shows Joseph as having been born in Westerleigh, and although Joseph was actually born in the Chipping Sodbury Union Workhouse at Yate, the fact that his mother Hannah was there as a 'guest' of the Westerleigh Parish gave her son a Westerleigh domicile.

Life as a farm servant was likely to have been hard work, as most employers of workhouse paupers got as much out of them as they could, and few cared how such children fared. The Chipping Sodbury Union records show that in 1854, Mr. Croome, the workhouse Master, was accused by five paupers of giving short rations, an accusation which fell on deaf ears, but in 1856 the Master was convicted of unlawfully assaulting and beating an adult, William Dyer, and confining him to a cell for ten hours. So, not only the children suffered, as was clearly illustrated contemporaneously by Charles Dickens, but also the adults. On balance the workhouse pauper was probably better off working at a farm, as there is a good possibility that the food was better than in the workhouse, and there was always the chance of finding a more kindly master than the workhouse beadle.

The probability is that as Joseph got older he would at times have lived at the farm, probably sleeping in the barn, or in a corner of a room, and it is unlikely that he would have been afforded much comfort. His labour would to an extent have depended on his physical capabilities, but he was likely to have been worked to his limit, fetching and carrying, bird-scaring, mucking out and feeding animals. During the summer months he would probably have been given a home-made overall type sacking smock to cover his breeches and gaiters or leggings. In winter the smock would have been more waterproof. The farmer would almost certainly still be wearing breeches to his knees with stockings or gaiters, as trousers, now in fashion in the towns and cities, had not yet penetrated into the countryside. Most probably sacks tied around the knees and down to the boots would protect the legs.

We have at this point a curious situation that would have caused the young Joseph a personal problem, and perhaps some embarrassment. Consider the position of a nine or ten year old boy, brought up in a workhouse, which, contrary to the general situation in the countryside at that time actually had WCs. Farms at that time might have had a 'privy' set over a hole in the ground, an earth closet with a renewable earth box, or certainly in the case of labourers' cottages, convenient hedgerows. Toilet paper in the form we now know it had not come into being, and newspaper was a luxury not known to all. After having known the W.C. at the workhouse, Joseph would almost certainly have been expected to find his own convenience at the farm. One can sympathize with his perplexity at the lack of 'wiping' facilities, which in established practice was accommodated by leaves, grass, smooth stones, sticks or fingers.

There is no way of telling whether Joseph worked at one farm, or many farms, or whether he had a variety of jobs, but somewhere between the 1861 Census and the 1871 Census Joseph managed to extricate himself from the workhouse system. There were several ways that he could have done this, but the most likely is that he showed the workhouse authorities that he could support himself, and need no longer be 'a burden on the Parish'. There are records of workhouse apprenticeships, but no indication that Joseph ever had this opportunity, so his most likely opportunity would have come from either a physical attribute, perhaps he was a very strong young man, or a natural attribute, such as ability with animals. If Joseph was offered job security from a source outside the workhouse he could then free himself of one of his handicaps.

Joseph was twenty years old when the 1871 Census was taken overnight on April 7th - 8th, although he is recorded as being twenty -one. He was working as an ostler for Thomas Hawking, and his wife Mary, at the White Hart, 9 Old Market Street, in the Parish of Philip and Jacob, Bristol. It is possible that it was a skill with horses that Joseph learned whilst working on the farm that gave him this opportunity. How Joseph was introduced to Mr. Hawking is not known, but the White Hart was a well-known coaching inn close to the market in Bristol, so possibly Joseph might have accompanied a farmer there on market days. Mr. Hawking had been established at the White Hart since at least as early as 1844, as he appears there in Pigot's Directory for that year. Living at the inn was Thomas Hawking's son, also Thomas, a commercial traveller, Thomas's thirty-year-old unmarried daughter Marianne, and Sarah Ann Morris, a thirty-five year old widow, both of whom were assistants in the business. There was also the unmarried domestic servant Mary Wadham, aged thirty-seven, from Taunton, and another domestic servant, Harriet Dyer, aged twenty-four, Joseph's wife to be. In fact Harriet was born on the 25th October 1849 at Iron Acton, so she was only twenty-one.

Harriet's life as a domestic servant up to this time would not have been easy. Apart from the amount of work and the long hours, she would also have been hampered by the fact that she might have worn a crinoline dress. The crinoline was the current fashion, and some female servants insisted on wearing the crinoline rather than be thought to be out of fashion. Not many servants were in a position to make such demands, but many employers would also not like to be thought to employ staff wearing old-fashioned clothes. The crinoline was a dress held away from the body by a series of fine steel hoops and cotton tapes, supporting petticoats. Apart from making it difficult to manoeuvre in confined spaces, and even to get through doorways, domestic servants were very prone to knocking over pieces of light furniture and ornaments.

The Crinoline

Harriet's wage would be about four or five shillings a week, and a crinoline dress, which would last her about a year, would have cost her about ten or eleven shillings, or just the replacement dress to go over the hoops, about five or six shillings. A nine-inch loose cover hem, which was removable and washable, protected the bottom of these floor length dresses.

On Sunday the 8th September 1872 Joseph and Harriet were married at the Parish Church of St. Jude, Bristol.

The isle of St. Jude's Church, down which Joseph and Harriet would have walked on the 8th of September 1872.

On the marriage certificate Joseph and Harriet are stated to be living in Lamb St., the street in which the church stood. Joseph is shown as a brewer, but Harriet does not give an occupation, so perhaps she had left the White Hart when Joseph moved into brewing. Harriet stated her age to be twenty-three, one year less than she stated over a year earlier at the Census; even so she was still only twenty-two. Joseph, unlike many people in his situation, did not invent a father on the marriage certificate, but filled the space for his father with a '?'. There is no record of Joseph ever being connected with brewing, other than working at the White Hart, which is perhaps a little remote, and it seems quite a jump from ostler in April 1871 to a brewer in September 1872. There was, however, a brewery within two hundred yards of the White Hart, and there is a later connection with this industry, so at some point between April 1871 and September 1872 Joseph changed from being an ostler to an involvement in the brewing industry. Clearly Joseph had benefited from some education, as both he and Harriet were able to sign their names on the marriage certificate.

It would be interesting to know who was present at the wedding, and whether Joseph's mother Hannah, or his sisters, Mary Ann or Georgina, knew of the marriage. We do know that Alfred William Basher and Ellen Griffiths were there as witnesses, but they might have been Church Wardens, friends of the bride or groom, or colleagues from work.

We know something about Harriet Dyer's family from the 1851 Census. They lived at Acton Common, Iron Acton, Harriet being one year old; her father George was a coal miner, and her mother was formerly Mary Mills. According to the Census Harriet had two sisters, Elizabeth, aged fourteen, and Rhoda aged six, also three brothers, James aged twelve, George aged eleven, and Pharaoh aged eight, all of whom were coal miners. In fact Pharaoh was born in the summer of 1844, so he was only six years old when the Census was taken at the end of March 1851. Although the Mines and Collieries Act of 1842 had made it illegal for girls and boys of under ten years of age to work underground, evidence suggests that there was a large-scale breach of the law. Not only were children under ten years old illegally working in the mines, but Pharaoh's parents were stating so to the Census Enumerator! Joseph's work on the farm would have been hard, but he had at least avoided going down the mine like the infant Pharaoh

Between the times of Joseph and Harriet's wedding in September 1872, and the arrival of their first child in June 1873, they moved to Cardiff. Initially there seemed to be no obvious motive for the move, other than perhaps to make a clean break and start their married life in fresh surroundings free from the shadow of the workhouse. In fact Cardiff would not have been a surprising choice for a young couple wishing to make a break. Over the preceding twenty years Cardiff had usurped Bristol as the commercial centre for the south of Wales, was by this time the largest town in south Wales, and within the next decade was to overtake the north east of England as Britain's major coal exporter. From Bristol, Cardiff would have looked like a splendid land of opportunity. The town of Cardiff, as it was then, had spread over three decades from the Castle, and the old boroughs of St. John and St. Mary, as its centre, southwards towards the docks, and by the time Joseph and Harriet moved there it had also spread easterly to Roath, and westerly to Canton.

There was, however, another incentive for the young couple to go to Cardiff, that is, the presence there of Harriet's elder brother, Pharaoh. The records show that on the 11th April 1868 the twenty-three year old Pharaoh, now a blacksmith, married Elizabeth Ann Slade, aged twenty, at the Register Office in Cardiff. Pharaoh's address was given as 6 Adam Street, and Elizabeth's as 23 Union Street, her father being recorded as a 'sawyer', which is a man who saws wood, possibly cutting pit props for the South Wales coalfields. There is no known previous connection between Pharaoh and South Wales, but there is a speculative reason for Pharaoh's move, although it might be a little remote. In 1827 Mark and John Dyer were tried for maliciously shooting at Thomas Mills at Yate on the 24th October 1826. They were found guilty and hanged on Saturday 28th April 1827. There was a third Dyer, William, who escaped abroad, and together with a number of other locals the Dyers formed a part of the notorious Wickwar Gang, who had terrorised the neighbourhood for many years. Wickwar is a village five miles from Pharaoh's village of Iron Acton. Mark Dyer probably lived in Dyers Lane, Iron Acton, (which later became Acton Lane), and John lived in Clay Lane, Iron Acton (which later became Mission Road). At the time of Pharaoh's birth there were five families of Dyers living in Clay Lane, including Pharaoh and Harriet's family, and, although this was nearly twenty years after the hanging of five members of the Wickwar Gang, there is a strong possibility that the name "Dyer" was not regarded in very high esteem. This might have been some incentive for Pharaoh to try his luck in Cardiff.

Above and below, Clay Lane, Iron Acton, now Mission Road, as it is in the year 2002. Probably Joseph, Harriet, or even the Wickwar Gang, would still recognise parts of the lane.

As has been stated above, Harriet and Joseph were married at Bristol on Sunday the 8th September 1872. Pharaoh's wife Elizabeth had died in Cardiff at the end of 1870, and Pharaoh had returned to Bristol and remarried on the 24th November 1872 at Holy Trinity Church. His new bride was Mary Drinkwater, who coincidentally, in view of what is written above, came from the village of Wickwar. Pharaoh and Mary did, however, return to Cardiff where their first child was born in 1873. At the time of their marriage Pharaoh, still a blacksmith, gave an address in West Street, Bristol, and Mary was recorded as a twenty-year old servant living in Stapleton Road, Bristol. Incidentally, at the wedding Pharaoh reduced his age by three years for the records. The Bristol addresses given by Joseph and Harriet, and Pharaoh and Mary are all within a hundred yards or so of each other in the centre of the City, and their addresses in Cardiff in 1873 are less than half a mile apart, so it is probable that two couples went to Cardiff together.

Although the name Pharaoh is not a common name in modern times it was not uncommon in the middle of the nineteenth century. It can be assumed that the Pharaoh of our story was named after another Pharaoh Dyer who died in Iron Acton in October 1839, aged twenty-four, who was probably an uncle. There was also a Pharaoh Dyer living in Essex at this time who appears to be unrelated.

As we shall see later there was a continued contact between the Smallcombe family of Cardiff and the Dyers of Iron Acton.

# Chapter Two

## Joseph starts work in Cardiff.
### 1872 - 1884

Joseph and Harriet's first home in Cardiff was in all probability a shared home with another family. Three quarters of the houses in Victorian Cardiff were built after 1871, mainly on land provided by the major estate holders of Bute, Tredegar and Windsor. Due to the system of ninety-nine year ground leases, which entailed roads and sewers being built by the landowners and above average construction, the rents were considerably higher than in other parts of south Wales. Most houses were out of reach of the working class family, and tenants rented and took in lodgers to share the rent. At the time Joseph and Harriet moved to Cardiff the bulk of the rentals fell between seven-and-sixpence and thirteen-shillings per week, compared to a figure between six-shillings and seven-and-sixpence for the areas around Pontypridd and the Rhonda. This resulted in there being an average of seven people living in each house in Cardiff at that time, so it would be surprising if Joseph and Harriet had a house to themselves, particularly bearing in mind Joseph's earnings as a labourer, which at best would be about one pound a week.

Once settled in Cardiff Joseph's life is quite well documented. Joseph and Harriet's first child was, perhaps significantly, Harriet Hannah, who was born on Friday the 6th June 1873 at the family home, 11 Eclipse Street, Roath, Cardiff, which is about half a mile north of the Cardiff Docks. Joseph was recorded as a labourer, although there are no further details of his occupation. One wonders if Joseph's mother, Hannah, was aware of her first granddaughter, and namesake. On Wednesday the 25th June, just over two weeks after her birth, Harriet Hannah was baptised at All Saints Parish Church, Tyndall Street, Adamstown.

On the 1st September 1873 Joseph's brother-in-law Pharaoh Dyer, still a blacksmith, and his wife Mary Drinkwater had their first child, Thomas Pharaoh, at 22 Bedford Street, Cardiff, less than half a mile from Eclipse Street.

By Monday the 1st March 1875 Joseph and his family had moved from number 11 to number 9 Eclipse Street, where Rhoda, named after Harriet's elder sister, was born. Joseph was still labouring. Once more, just over two weeks after Rhoda was born, she was baptised at the same church as her sister, again on a Wednesday, the 17th March.

Numbers 9 and 11 Eclipse Street are to all intents and purposes identical. Number 11, shown here, having the front door on the right, and number 9 having the front door on the left.

Amazingly, two weeks after Rhoda was born to Joseph and Harriet, Joseph's mother Hannah produced his twin brother and sister, Harry and Eliza in Scarborough, her 7th and 8th illegitimate children.

In 1876 and 1877 Joseph and his family were to be found at 93 Clifton Street, but by the time Joseph and Harriet's first son Frederick Joseph was born on Sunday the 23rd of September 1877 Joseph had become a cab driver, and they were living at 73 Elm Street, Roath. Clifton Street was a quarter of a mile east of Eclipse Street, and Elm Street was a quarter of a mile north west of Clifton Street, so the family were moving within a very limited area, moving away from, but still within a mile of the docks. Yet again Joseph and Harriet had their latest offspring baptised at the same church, on Wednesday the 17th October, three weeks after the birth.

Joseph is not listed in any local directories as being a cab driver or proprietor, so possibly he was an employee, or he just did not claim an entry in a directory. The 'cab' that Joseph drove would have been one of two sorts, either the 'growler' a cab for four persons, or the two wheeled hansom cab, which normally catered for two persons. The hansom cab is probably the better known and more popular cab, in which the cabbie sat high up at the rear with the reins running over the top of the cab, taking instructions through a small trap door in the roof.

The Hansom cab, with bowler hated cabbie who had replaced the earlier city cabbie in the top hat. The 'bowler' was developed in 1850 and took the Bowler name in 1860. The top hat had run out of fashion by the end of the nineteenth century.

Perhaps it is not inappropriate to explain a little about the form of these various vehicles. Originally the four wheeled, two-horse hackney coach was the main form of city transport. The French cabriolet was adapted in England as a two-wheeled one horse 'cab' for public transport in the 1820s, and the hansom cab form of this was developed by the 1830s. The hansom cab became the main means of fast communication in the cities, such as London, whereas the hackney coach was used for slower and heavier loads, such as transporting more than two persons, and passengers with luggage, as the railways developed from the 1840s.

Setting up, running and maintaining the hansom cab cost about twice as much as that required for a hackney coach, partly because of the need for fitter, faster, more surefooted horses. Unfortunately the working life of the hansom cab horse, and its necessary reserve horse, was shorter than that of its coach counterpart, and in any event the mortality rate for these horses was quite high, particularly in winter with the necessity for standing around in rain and snow, and then suddenly being put to hard fast work on city cobbles. It is possible that the cab Joseph drove might have had rubber tyres fitted to it as they had been introduced quite recently, although they were not used on the four-wheeled coaches. Although it comes beyond Joseph's working days as a cabbie, an interesting piece of historical information should be mentioned here. There had always been problems on fare assessment and pricing, but just at the very end of the nineteenth century a system of taximeters was introduced, to record the distance and fare. Horse drawn cabs were not compelled to fit them, but the recent internal combustion cabs were so compelled, these became known as taxicabs, a name which persists to the present day. Once the telephone, telegraph and other means of more modern communication became commonplace the hansom cab declined in places such as London, but in the provinces the decline was slower and governed more by the development of public transport, such as trams and buses.

It is not known for whom Joseph drove his cab, or where he picked up his fares, but he lived about midway between the docks and the new Maindy Barracks. The barracks were completed in 1877 and occupied by the 24th Sub District Brigade Headquarters, and the Permanent Staff of the Royal Glamorgan Militia. The Militia were to

17

use the Maindy Field, adjacent to the barracks, for annual training under canvas until as late as 1894. So, presumably the docks and the military provided Joseph with a fair proportion of his income.

The records show that by the late 1880s there were one hundred and fifty licensed cabs in Cardiff, and there were public cab stands at the Town Hall, Bute Docks, Queen Street, Bute Terrace, Gaol Lane, Wood Street, Royal Hotel, Westgate Street and Elm Street. (Gaol Lane was renamed in 1936, and became Knox Road, named after John Simpson Knox, formerly of the King's Rifle Brigade, and an 1880s Governor of the adjacent prison). Although the hansom cab was to survive for some time yet, the first local threat had appeared in 1872 in the form of the first horse drawn tram. By 1878 the tram had reached Roath and Canton, and by 1881 had reached Grangetown. It was, however, to be another two decades before it would become electrified in Cardiff, and at least three decades before the motor taxicab superseded its horse drawn competition.

This horse drawn tram is on the Roath to the Docks route.

We must not overlook, however, the day-to-day problems of the transport system of the time. As the second half of the twentieth century had to cope with the problems of traffic congestion and pollution, so too did the second half of the nineteenth century. I recall my grandmother reminiscing about her youth towards the end of the nineteenth century, and commenting about the horrendous traffic jams around the east end of London, caused by the horse drawn vehicles. Contemporary photographs and paintings confirm this view. This can also be supported by the fact that the official allowance for cab ranks was fifteen feet (five metres) for a horse drawn vehicle, and nine feet (three metres) for a motor taxicab. As to the twentieth century problems of carbon dioxide emission, these were matched by the methane emission produced in the nineteenth century by the three million tons of horse manure deposited on the streets annually by the one horsepower cab.

To return to Joseph, this was a very important period for him. He appears on the Electoral Rolls for 1877 and 1878, which were compiled on the 1st November each year, and included any men owning property worth more than fifty pounds per annum, or renting property worth more than twelve pounds per annum, that is just over four and sixpence a week. This is the first time Joseph appears on the Electoral Roll, and indicates that he had by this time moved a little up the social ladder, probably because he now rented his own house, rather than living as a lodger in the houses of others. The Electoral Roll shows the family living at 13 Lily Street, one street north of Elm Street, so the family must have moved from 73 Elm Street to 13 Lily Street between the birth of Frederick Joseph on the 23rd September 1877, and the compilation of the Electoral Roll on the 1st November 1877.

We should not miss the significance of this part of Joseph's life, because the dates and addresses do not impart the probable human story behind the facts. As Joseph's story unfolds it will become apparent that he was probably an opportunist, and due to his pauper background, pennywise. This does not imply that he was mean, but that he was probably acutely aware of the value of money, and he might well have been able to save money from his labouring wage, more so than many in his position. It is true to say that Joseph did have a reputation within the family for being thrifty.

It is known that Joseph was a labourer on the 1st March 1875 at 9 Eclipse Street, and also that he was a cab driver by the 23rd September 1877 at 73 Elm Street. It is probably not a coincidence that there was a cab rank in Elm Street. It needs little imagination to see this enterprising twenty-seven year old labourer talking to cabbies, particularly bearing in mind his previous occupation as an ostler, and finding a way into the business.

There were several means of earning a living as a cabbie. One could purchase a new or second hand rig and work as an owner-driver, become an employed cab driver, or hire a cab at ten-shillings to fifteen-shillings per day from a cab owner. In the provinces the cabbies generally worked for a cab proprietor who paid them a wage, to which was added any tips that the cabbie might earn. Joseph's earnings as a cabbie would depend on how many hours he worked, rather than the fixed wage for fixed hours as a labourer, and some cabbies were known to work a 16 hour day for thirteen days in a fortnight.

Joseph's move from 73 Elm Street to 13 Lily Street might be very significant, because 13 Lily Street had two sets of double gates leading to a yard at the rear, with a building that was almost certainly used as a coach house and stables.

13 Lily Street

The Blue House, a mews house behind the doors of 13 Lily Street, almost certainly used by Joseph at some time to stable his horses.

There is a possibility that Joseph, who could possibly have been a cabbie for anything up to two and a half years before moving to 13 Lily Street, might have been able to purchase his own rig. At this time a hansom cab would have cost Joseph about seventy pounds, he would need two horses, costing between eight pounds and twenty pounds each, about five pounds for accessories, and the two pounds five-shillings for the cab licence, a total of about one hundred pounds. This would be at least two years wages for a labourer. If Joseph had stabling at his home, that would save a considerable sum in weekly expenses, and Joseph's experience on the farm as a youngster, and at the White Hart in Bristol would stand him in good stead. As a cabbie Joseph might have known an old cabbie, who wanted to retire, or someone forced to give up driving, or he might have known someone prepared to lend him some capital to get him started. (It was similar opportunist circumstances that propelled my own father into business). Financially, Joseph would be much better off if he could have afforded to go into business on his own account. The owner-driver would have to deduct his costs of maintenance from his takings, and the cost of feed and bedding for two horses would have been about ten-shillings a week each. The dates show

21

that it was possible that Joseph could have remained at 13 Lily Street, as a cab owner-driver for two years before moving on again.

One wonders at this point whether Joseph had by now developed a plan, or whether again opportunism guided his fate, but it should be remembered that when Joseph married he had moved from being an ostler, into the brewing business.

The family left 13 Lily Street at some time after the 1st November 1878, when the electoral roll was compiled, to 65 Sandon Terrace, St. John, where their daughter Beatrice was born on Thursday the 23rd October 1879. Joseph and Harriet changed the established pattern of baptisms for Beatrice as she was baptised on Monday the 17th November, albeit at the same church as her siblings, three weeks after she was born. Joseph was by now a barman, and the Electoral Rolls for 1879 to 1881 show the family living at 65 Adam Street.

At this point the geographical situation of these addresses must be clarified. Adam Street was within a quarter mile of the dock gates, and about three quarters of a mile S.W. of Lily Street, and evidence from the Electoral Registers, Street and Name Directories, the 1881 Census, contemporary photographs, and birth certificates, indicate that 65 Sandon Terrace, only referred to on one birth certificate, 65 Adam Street, and the Sandon Hotel were all one building. Backing onto the properties numbered 65 to 87 Adam Street, was Sandon Place, which ran parallel to Adam Street, and into Sandon Street, which in turn joined Adam Street at a junction upon which the Sandon Hotel was situated. It is possible that the Sandon Hotel had an annex that claimed the number 65, whilst the hotel used the number 65A. It would make sense that Joseph and the family were living at this address because Joseph was the barman at the Sandon Hotel. Backing onto the Sandon Hotel was a lodging house, number 1 Sandon Place situated at the corner of Sandon Place and Sandon Street. It is possible that it was this gap in Sandon Street, between this lodging house and the Sandon Hotel, which was the annex. It has to be said, however, that this hypothesis is not conclusive, as Joseph, as will be seen shortly, had a lodger at number 65.

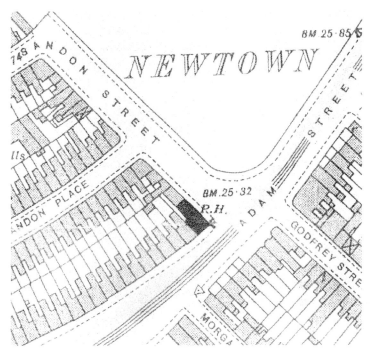

The blacked in section at the corner of Sandon Street and Adam Street is the Sandon Hotel. The probable position of the annex behind the hotel can be clearly seen. The clear area marked "Newtown" is His Majesty's Prison.

In the six years between 1872 and 1878 Joseph, Harriet, and their family had lived at six different addresses, and Joseph had been a labourer, a cab driver, and a barman. Yet again we are drawn to the conclusion that many of these moves were probably due to the family living as boarders in the homes of others, but this was to change.

This latest move to 65 Adam Street took the family out of south Roath, which was an area noted as being primarily Irish and working class, into the ancient parish of St. John. Joseph and Harriet's neighbours, apart from the hotel and lodging house in which dwelt three charwomen, were a shoemaker, a dock labourer, a baker's shop, a 'fire and house agent' and his family, a house decorator, and a Friendly Society Agent, so the area was still working class.

Apart from their day to day lives, we should not forget that Joseph and Harriet were living in times of expansion and colonialism, and although they were busy with the family, and earning a living, they could not be unaware of the worldwide matters going on around them, which in one way or another could affect their lives and the lives of those with whom they came into contact, particularly with the docks so close by. Britain at this time was a powerful Colonial power and a great deal of what went on abroad affected the country as a whole. The year 1879 saw the start of the Zulu War in South Africa, which would feature strongly in the newspapers of the time, particularly with the local military presence.

The year 1881 looks like a turning point in Joseph's life. By the time of the Census, taken overnight on April 3/4th, Joseph, the barman would have been thirty, and was so recorded, and Harriet, now thirty-one was also recorded as thirty. Harriet clearly had the knack of reducing her age gently as the years passed, not, however, to the extent that Joseph's mother did as can be seen in another story. The Census not only shows the family at home at 65 Adam Street, including daughters Harriet Hannah, aged seven, Rhoda aged six, Beatrice aged one, and son Frederick Joseph aged three, but within that same household are to be found Elizabeth Brown, a servant born in Cardiff, aged twelve, and Harold Agg, a lodger and student aged eleven, from Pontypool. Harold Agg was probably the son of forty-nine year old widower Thomas Agg, a porter from the nearby Newport Road Infirmary. It is possible that Thomas Agg also lived with Joseph and Harriet, but was at the hospital at the time the Census was recorded. Elizabeth Brown was clearly a servant to Joseph and Harriet because her relationship to Joseph is recorded as a 'servant', as well as her occupation being recorded as 'servant'.

Joseph and Harriet having a servant is quite a surprise because Joseph as a barman did not seem to be of such status as would normally be expected to keep a servant. It does, however, give us some insight as to Joseph's position, as it is reasonably well established that it was necessary to have an income of at least one hundred and fifty pounds per annum to sustain a servant. This sum was probably about fifty percent higher than the wage of a skilled manual worker of the time, but Joseph was probably careful to husband his tips as a barman. It is possible that Elizabeth Brown was an ex-workhouse girl, to whom Joseph gave employment with considerable recognition of his former estate, or perhaps she was just a young girl in service from a working class background. As a twelve year old she would only have been earning five pounds per annum all -found, or half that sum if she were a workhouse girl.

This is not, however, the end of this particular saga. The Census reveals another household also living at 65 Adam Street, that of the Ridgwoods. John Ridgwood, the head, was a mason aged twenty-eight, his wife Sarah was twenty-seven, son Thomas was eight, daughter Sarah was six, and son John was four. This perhaps supports the hypothesis that the property was an annex to the hotel, perhaps used as a lodging house, although by modern day standards the number of people who could live in one small house at any one time beggars belief.

On Monday the 1st August 1881 Joseph and Harriet's second son, William Albert Jones Smallcombe, was born at 65 Adam Street, St. John, and Joseph was still a barman. The choice of names for his son initially looks curious. It was not uncommon for surnames to be used as a second forename, but this was usually the mother's maiden name, or, if a child was illegitimate it was a means of indicating who the father might be. In this case the choice of 'Jones' as a forename is not Harriet's maiden name, and surely it cannot indicate illegitimacy! It would seem most unlikely that a married couple would wish to wash their dirty linen in public, so to speak, unless perhaps the husband had a particularly vindictive mind, and felt no shame in so exposing his wife. A more charitable view would be that Jones was the name of a close friend being honoured by the family, but at first glances this seems a little unlikely, as Joseph and Harriet would be aware of the implications. It seems probable, however, that this latter explanation might be correct, as the licensee of the Sandon Hotel was William Jones, but perhaps of more significance is the fact that his wife Henrietta was born in Yate, the same village as Joseph and the next village to where Harriet was born. There might even be a stronger connection as William Jones at the Census was thirty eight years old, and Henrietta was forty six, so it is possible that this was a second marriage and there might even have been a connection with the former spouses of either party. Even then there is a twist to the tale. This is the only child of Joseph and Harriet for whom a baptism has not been found, and, as will be seen, more anomalies were to follow.

One event abroad that would have made the newspapers in that year was the British involvement in the protection of the Suez Canal. Joseph would have been nineteen when the Suez Canal, connecting the Mediterranean and Red Seas, was opened in 1869 shortening the very important trade routes to India. In 1882 an uprising by the Egyptian Army put the security of these trade routes into jeopardy, and Major General Wolsey was sent to take control of the situation and subsequently Egypt itself. Whilst on the subject of the military, the previously mentioned Maindy Barracks was to see an historic event in 1881, when the 1st Battalion The Welch Regiment (41st Foot) amalgamated with the 1st Battalion The South Lincolnshire Regiment (69th Foot), having relocated from Fort Hubbertson, Pembrokeshire, to form The Welch Regiment (41st/69th Foot).

On the 1882 Electoral Roll, Joseph and Harriet are still at 65 Adam Street, now having been four years at this address. By Tuesday the 15th May 1883, however, when Florence Blanche was born, the family was living at 88 Adam Street, and Joseph had now become a club manager, having been a barman for about four years since moving into 65 Adam Street. It cannot be ascertained whether this address was the club at which Joseph worked or not, as all the evidence points to the fact that the numbers in Adam Street only went up to 87. As with the other children, except William Albert Jones, Florence was baptised three weeks after her birth at the same Church in Tyndall Street, reverting again to a Wednesday, the 6th of June.

The post of club manager might have been temporary however, as Joseph is recorded as a barman again on Friday the 3rd October 1884 when daughter Alice Maud Mary was born at 88 Adam Street. On the other hand perhaps Joseph merely recorded his occupation as 'barman' whilst still at the club. There might, however, be a simple explanation for the change from the hotel to a 'club'. In 1881 the "Welsh Sunday Closing Act" came into being with pressure from the temperance and sabbatarianism lobbies. The Act was not unanimously welcome in Cardiff, and many drinking clubs opened in order to get round the Act. In 1881 Cardiff had one drinking club, by 1883, when Joseph became a 'club manager' there were thirteen drinking clubs, by 1886 this had expanded to one hundred and forty one. It is probably that the Sandon Hotel extended its operations to a drinking club further down Adam Street.

Alice Maud was baptised at the same church as her brother and sisters, but unfortunately the date was not recorded in the Church records. It was certainly between the entries either side of it, dated 15th October and December 14th, so as Joseph was such a creature of habit, one could guess that it was probably Wednesday 22nd October.

All Saints Church, Tyndall Street.

As will be seen Joseph's jobs as barman and club manager had prepared him for his next move.

# Chapter Three

### Joseph strikes out on his own.
### 1885

This Chapter covers Joseph's first steps from the relative security of an employed person into the less secure status of a self-employed person.

On the 5th January 1885 Joseph became independent, and became the licensee of the Westgate Hotel at 49 Cowbridge Road, owned by Mrs. Thomas of 48 Cowbridge Road. The Westgate Hotel was, and the rebuilt Westgate Hotel still is, on the corner of Cowbridge Road and Lower Cathedral Road, in the Parish of St. Mary. This was the furthest the family had moved since Joseph and Harriet had arrived in Cardiff, and was about three quarters of a mile from their previous abode in Adam Street. The area behind the Westgate Hotel towards the docks was still being developed, and an 1883 map shows Lower Cathedral Road running into Brook Street, two hundred yards from the Westgate Hotel, which was at the end of the development at that time. A road called Moor Road appears to be the road which eventually was to become Clare Street and Clare Road.

The Westgate Hotel, probably taken 1911

28

The move to the Westgate Hotel marked the start of life in the second of the three distinctive areas in which the family were to live, and for the children there was a bonus of being immediately opposite Sophia Gardens and Bute Park, which were divided by the River Taff. At the time of the 1881 Census the Westgate Hotel was being managed by an unmarried thirty-seven year old lady, Louisa Griffiths, living with her sixteen year old niece Florence Seager, but Joseph takes the licence, and is not merely a manager.

Sophia Garden about 1911

On Thursday the 17th December 1885 Harriet gave birth to Lily Ada, their sixth daughter, their eighth and last child, at the Westgate Hotel. She was baptised at the usual church, on Wednesday 13th January, four weeks after her birth. Harriet was by now thirty-six, and Joseph thirty-five. This probably threw their Christmas preparations into confusion, although Harriet Hannah was twelve years old, and as with girls of that age at that time, well able to help out. Many girls of Harriet Hannah's age would have already been working as servants.

To get a feel for Joseph's way of life it is sometimes necessary to put him into his historical context. Until Joseph arrived in Cardiff he had probably not lived anywhere that had been lit by anything other

29

than candles, certainly the workhouse in Chipping Sodbury did not have gas installed until after 1870. This move into the Westgate Hotel was probably Joseph's first experience of gaslight, and possibly during his occupation of the Westgate he might have changed the flickering gas lamps for the newly invented incandescent gas mantle, which gave a much brighter more constant light. It is also possible that Joseph might have died, nearly forty years later, never having used electric light.

As for Harriet, looking after a family of eight children and a husband was no easy task as there were few mechanical aids for the housewife of those days. Early every morning the coal fired kitchen range had to be lit, after having been cleaned and blacked, and the coalscuttle would have to be filled from the outdoor coalbunker. The rest of the house probably would not have been heated unless someone was sick, in which case the small bedroom fire might have been lit, but there might have been a fire to light in the bar.

The kitchen range would have heated pans of water for cooking and washing. There would probably have been a separate 'copper' for heating water for washing clothes, a long and very laborious job, the frequency of which was dictated by the amount of linen and clothes available, and the number of persons in the house. In many cases washday occurred every three, four, or even five weeks, and took at least two full days, but sometimes necessity dictated that it would be a weekly event. Clothes were put in hot water to soak or boil, pounded and stirred with a washing 'dolly' in soapy water, transferred to the scrubbing board by a copper-stick, for some vigorous rubbing up and down the corrugated metal surface, then rinsed. The clothes would then be put through the rollers of a mangle to extract the water, and finally hung out to dry on the clothesline held between two stout posts in the garden or yard. This in itself was hazardous as soot from the coal fires was a constant problem, and many a good tempered housewife had her patience tested to the limit with smuts of soot on freshly washed linen. When the clothes or linen were sufficiently dry they would be taken indoors and the flat irons, which had been heating on the top of the range, would be used to iron out the creases. Even though this would take at least a full day Hannah would still have to feed herself, her husband, and eight hungry children.

Shopping was a more time consuming task than it is in modern society as refrigerators had not been invented, and the less efficient iceboxes with manufactured ice were the only means of cooling food. The housewife also had to resort to pickling and preserving as part of her culinary activities because many foods were not available all the year round as is now the case. Other household chores were unbelievably time consuming compared to modern days, and the children would have been expected to help with a great number of household chores that are completely unknown today.

There was, however, some good news for the housewife as far as food and fashion were concerned. Due to improvements in refrigeration, packaging, and marketing, the cost of the family food basket of bread, butter, tea, milk and meat, dropped by almost a third between 1877 and 1889. Also, women's fashions had changed and the crinoline had been replaced by the bustle, a flat fronted dress bunched up behind, supported by a small whalebone cage tied with tapes around the waist.

Although Joseph had suffered a deprived and hard childhood, he had not been directly affected by personal tragedy. Having said that, three of his siblings had died in the workhouse as infants. Edmund died at nine months old when Joseph was six; Charlotte Eliza died aged fifteen months when Joseph was thirteen, and Henry Tilling Smallcombe died at four years of age when Joseph was nineteen, but it is not known to what extent Joseph was aware of these births or deaths.

Personal tragedy did, however, strike the family for the first time on Friday the 18th June 1886, when Lily Ada died aged six months, at 89 Cowbridge Road, Canton, of asphyxia, having been ill with catarrh for five days. It must have been an agonizing death, and agonizing for the parents to watch. It is not unusual for the comment to be made concerning infant deaths, that 'this was a very frequent occurrence in Victorian families', but this does not make the individual's grief and pain any the less. Joseph and Harriet would have felt no differently to the way we would feel today about the loss of a child and loved one.

No explanation has been found for Lily dying at 89 Cowbridge Road, Canton. It was never one of Joseph's addresses, and the family were living at the Westgate Hotel at this time. The occupier of 89

Cowbridge Road in 1886/7 was a James Fraser, a Dock master, and he still occupied the premises in 1893, by which time it was known as Ninian House. It might not be a coincidence that 89 Cowbridge Road was opposite the Cardiff Union Workhouse at 30 Cowbridge Road, known as City Lodge after 1914, and which became St. David's Hospital in 1948. There may yet be a further clue as to the use of 89 Cowbridge Road, as it is known that towards the end of the century the workhouse used what they described as 'Scattered Houses', presumably these were houses outside the parameters of the workhouse which might have been used for special cases, perhaps even as small hospitals or care centres. During the nineteenth century it was common for workhouses to act as local hospitals, and Joseph would be well aware of this.

The mysterious 89 Cowbridge Road

Lily Ada's death certificate shows that M. Quinn of 4 Bute Street was present at the death, and Joseph is shown as a publican, although on the burial order he is shown as a hotelkeeper. M. Quinn registered the death on the same day, but no direct connection has been found with Joseph's family and M. Quinn. One peculiarity of the situation concerning Lily Ada's death is that up to 1883 Harriet had registered the births of all of the children, and after 1883 Joseph registered the births and deaths of all of the children, except this one. It strikes a discordant note that Joseph and Harriet should allow a non-family member to register the death, unless perhaps that person held some official position. On the other hand, it was the first death that Harriet and Joseph had experienced in their family and perhaps it was just too much for them, more probably it supports the hypothesis that M. Quinn was a member of staff of the Cardiff Union.

On the day of Lily Ada's death, Friday 18th June 1886, Mr. Marsh the Funeral Director was contacted, and he purchased a grave on behalf of the family. On Monday the 21st June at 12 noon, Lily Ada was buried in grave number 183 in section 'L' of Cathays Cemetery.

This 1904 picture postcard shows the entrance and Chapel at Cathays Cemetery, which was to become an all too familiar sight to Joseph and Harriet over the next few years.

33

Returning to the question of M. Quinn, the 1881 Census shows three M. Quinn, the first being Mary, the thirteen-year-old daughter of Thomas Quinn of 9 Herbert Street, Cardiff. Herbert Street is close to Adam Street, where the Smallcombe family lived only the previous year, and Mary would have been eighteen at the time of Lily Ada's death. Peculiarly enough there is another Mary Quinn also living at 9 Herbert Street, a twenty six year old charwoman living as a lodger with the Collins family, and she would have been thirty-one at the time of Lily Ada's death. There is yet a third contender for the attendant at Lily Ada's death, Margaret Quinn, a domestic servant and the step daughter of Andrew Drew of 15 Ellen Street, again just around the corner from the Smallcombe family's former residence in Adam Street; Margaret would have been twenty nine at the time of Lily Ada's death. It is possible that whoever it was, she was working at the Westgate Hotel as a 'domestic', or a 'charwoman', but that doesn't relate to the address of 89 Cowbridge Road. There is a further clue, however, in that the Slater's Directories for 1882-1891 show a Mary Quinn, a nurse, living at 4 Kyte Street, which was later Kite Street, which no longer exists but was roughly where Davis Street is today. So, in all probability one Mary Quinn of the 1881 Census became a nurse, and possibly she worked at 89 Cowbridge Road by 1886.

On the left is the Cardiff Union Workhouse in Cowbridge Road.
The road on the right would have taken Joseph to Clare Road.
About fifty yards past that turning is 89 Cowbridge Road.

34

The Cardiff Union Workhouse, with Alfred Greenhalgh the Master, and Margaret Parry Head Nurse, was only two hundred yards or so from the Westgate Hotel, and must have been a constant reminder to Joseph of his origins, and how far he had come. This workhouse was, however, much larger than the one Joseph knew at Chipping Sodbury. The Cardiff Union covered forty-two parishes, with a population of 106,164, and a rateable value of £1,183,161 at the 1881 Census. The average number of inmates at the workhouse and schools was nine hundred and twenty-four. The average cost of keeping an inmate at the workhouse, was four-shillings and four-pence (about twenty-two pence), and keeping a child at school was four-shillings and sixpence. The Board of Governors consisted in forty-one ex-officio members, and sixty-seven elected members, who met every Saturday at half past twelve in the afternoon.

One brighter event occurred in 1887 when Queen Victoria's Golden Jubilee was celebrated. Victoria had reigned for fifty years, and had been a widow for twenty-six of those years. In fact Victoria's prolonged period of mourning for Albert had caused no little concern for the Government and the people alike. Many considered that the Affairs of State were being neglected, and there was probably more republican feeling during this period than at any other time before or since.

Tragedy was to strike the family again just over two years later when the now youngest child, Alice Maud Mary aged four, died of measles and pneumonia at the Westgate Hotel, 49 Cowbridge Road, on Saturday the 20th October 1888. Her father Joseph was with her when she died, and he registered the death on the following Monday, the day of Alice's funeral. Once more the family made its way to the Cathays Cemetery, and Lily Ada's grave was opened for her elder sister to join her. Alice Maud was buried, again in the care of Mr. Marsh, on Monday the 22nd October at four o'clock in the afternoon.

# Chapter Four

## Expansion
## 1889-1900

Before continuing let us remind ourselves of Joseph's family at the start of 1889. Joseph was now thirty-eight years old, Harriet was thirty-nine, and they had been married for sixteen years. The rest of the family consisted of the children Harriet Hannah aged fifteen, Rhoda aged thirteen, Frederick Joseph aged eleven, Beatrice aged nine, William Albert Jones aged seven, and Florence Blanche aged five. Two children had already died, Lily Ada two years earlier aged six months, and Alice Maud Mary had been dead for three months, dying two weeks after her fourth birthday.

In the fashion of the day Harriet the housewife would just be dispensing of her wardrobe of dresses with bustles and starting to wear dresses which fitted tightly around the waist, that then spread to a bell shape at the floor. These were nowhere near as wide as the old crinoline, used half the old crinoline frame, and later developed fashionable billowing sleeves, called leg of mutton sleeves.

Men's fashions had varied little and were as dowdy as ever; top hats were still the fashion but being overtaken by the bowler in many spheres, frock coats, trousers, and black leather shoes still prevailed.

The story of Joseph and his family becomes very complicated at this point, as it appears that whilst Joseph was working as the landlord of the Westgate Hotel he decided to diversify. From 1886 to 1888 Joseph had described himself as a 'publican' on birth and death certificates, but in 1889 we have a dramatic new departure for Joseph and Harriet. The 1889 Directory lists for the first time H. F. Smallcombe, Mineral Water Manufacturer of 38 Clare Road, and Allerton Street, whilst Joseph was, of course, still at the Westgate Hotel.

This reference to Allerton Street in the 1889 Directory, probably compiled in 1888, is rather surprising as it was not until the 25th April 1890 that Joseph purchased a freehold plot from G and F Couzens in "a new road or street called Allerton Street". The mortgage document, from John Rees of 23 Cowbridge Road, dated the 26th April 1890, refers to the mortgage on a property "intended to be called Allerton Street".

It is probable that Joseph had purchased the plot of land in what was to become Allerton Street, to which he had access from 38 Clare Road. That access is still currently in use in the year 2002. The Allerton Street address at this time almost certainly refers to storage that was to become the yard facility behind number 12 Allerton Street, but probably the houses had not yet been built. Certainly there is evidence here of some expansion into the mineral water manufacturing business, and possibly 38 Clare Road was then a shop. It is interesting to note that next door to number 38 Clare Road, at number 36, lived Harriet Hornblow, whose son was to marry Joseph's daughter in two years time.

This is the third and final area move for Joseph and his family, originally from Roath then Canton or St. Mary's, and now to the area known variously as Grange, Grangetown, or Saltmead. Joseph and Harriet and family were to live in numerous houses in Clare Road during the next few decades.

Joseph and Harriet's houses in Clare Road were all similar terraced houses, the same in size as those in Eclipse Street. Sash windows were probably the original type of window; some properties have, or have had, shop fronts at some time.

Number 12 next to the double doors, and 14 Allerton Street on the left, were similar but with smaller rooms. Access to the room above the arch was by ladder.

This map shows the relationship between Joseph's houses in Clare Road, and the house and yard in Allerton Street. The main road is Clare Road, and the blanked in houses from the top are numbers 16, 32, 36, 38, and 46. On the opposite side of the road are numbers 35 and 67. The house and yard blacked out in Allerton Street is number 12 with the yard at the back. The gardens of 36 and 38 Clare Road back onto the Allerton Street yard. The garden of 32 backs onto the yard buildings.

There were two official designations for Joseph and Harriet's new sideline. Manufacturers were listed in trade journals as Mineral Water Manufacturers, and, or, as Aerated Water and Temperance Drinks Manufacturers. The latter designation seems not to be exclusive, and was adopted by manufacturers who manufactured carbonated waters as well as brewing beers. The Western Mail Cardiff Directories for 1887 to 1889 show Joseph as resident at the Westgate Hotel, 49 Cowbridge Road. As has been mentioned earlier Allerton Street, to be significant in Joseph's life a little later, was in the process of being built during the 1888-9 period, and the same applies to Clare Road, which only appears to have nine inhabited houses in the 1888-9 Directory.

It is clear that the name of the business was H. F. Smallcombe. There is, however, no record of an H. F. Smallcombe within the family, and it is assumed that the "HF" was a combination of Joseph's wife Harriet and their son Frederick Joseph. Frederick Joseph would have been twelve years old in September 1889, and his younger brother William Albert Jones would have been eight. One wonders if there is any significance in the fact that William Albert

39

Jones Smallcombe was not included in this deal, and why the business was not called HFW. If it is not significant, then perhaps William was considered too young to be included.

If the business had been put into Harriet's name, this would have been made possible by the Married Woman's Property Act of 1882, which enabled women for the first time to buy, own and sell property, and keep their own earnings.

The 1891 Census shows the family still at the Westgate Hotel, 49 Cowbridge Road, although the Resident's Directory shows it as 49 Westbourne Place, and Joseph is now shown as a Licensed Victualler. Harriet Hannah, and Rhoda are listed as barmaids, with Frederick aged 13, Beatrice aged 11, William aged 8, although he was actually 9, and Blanche aged 7, all listed as scholars. For some peculiar reason Joseph, now 40 is recorded as 37, and Harriet, although 41, is recorded as 38. It appears from this that the family's main concern was the Westgate Hotel, but that the sidelines were being developed in conjunction with the pub. The Western Mail Cardiff Directory does not list number 38 Clare Road in 1891, but it is probable that the mineral water business still used this address.

Whilst speaking of the 1891 Census and Joseph's family in a Chapter headed "Expansion", perhaps Joseph's brother-in-law Pharaoh Dyer warrants a mention. It might be recalled from Chapter Two that in 1873 Pharaoh had been a blacksmith living at 22 Bedford Street, Cardiff, with his wife Mary, and a son called Thomas Pharaoh. Since that time Pharaoh had moved to a private house at 107 Castle Road (later City Road), and expanded his business to become a wheelwright and smith at 103 Castle Road. By 1891 Pharaoh's family had moved to a terraced house at 38 Cyfartha St., only a hundred yards or so from his business premises in Castle Road. His family had also expanded and now consisted of himself, his wife Mary, the previously mentioned Thomas Pharaoh now aged seventeen, May sixteen, Maud fourteen, Florrie thirteen, Annie eleven, Harriet nine, Emily five, George four, and Clifford two. There was also a locally born nineteen-year-old domestic servant Annie Nibblett. Clearly expansion was not confined to Joseph and Harriet.

Perhaps a little unusually, it was on a Monday, the 27th July 1891, when Joseph and Harriet's eldest daughter Harriet Hannah married

William Hornblow at the Welsh Congregational Church, Canton, Cardiff. Harriet Hannah was eighteen, and gave her address as the Westgate Hotel, and William was a twenty two year old hydraulic attendant living at 9 Clare Road. As his mother Harriet Hornblow (Senior) was listed as the sole tenant of 36 Clare Road in 1889 it is probable that her husband Thomas was dead by that time. Harriet and William's marriage certificate, however, does shows Thomas Hornblow as William's father but does not show him as deceased. The witnesses on the certificate are Harriet's father Joseph and William's elder brother John Thomas Hornblow. Although Joseph was recorded on the marriage certificate as a wine and spirit merchant, he was still the licensee of the Westgate Hotel, but he relinquished his licence two weeks later, on the 5th August 1891.

Welsh Congregational Church, Severn Road, Canton

On birth and death certificates dated 1891 and 1892 Joseph described himself as a Wine and Spirit Merchant, so it would seem that this was indeed a new occupation and not merely an alternative description for his Westgate Hotel licence. The licence of the Westgate Hotel was subsequently taken by an R .P. Culley, and the following year it changed hands yet again and was taken by a Ruben Porter.

Although in the 1891 Western Mail Cardiff Directory Joseph is only shown at the Westgate Hotel, and indeed does not show again in that Directory until 1893-4, the 1891 edition of Kelly's South Wales Directory, takes up the story. In this directory we find Joseph at the Westgate Hotel, and

> "Smallcombe J. and Son, cordials manufacturers (all kinds)
> also wholesale beer, stout, cider & perry merchants, agents
> for Lane & Co.'s celebrated Irish stouts, 49 Westbourne pl.,
> Cowbridge road, Canton; works and factory, Saltmead."

This is the first comprehensive mention of Joseph's activities, the only mention of 49 Westbourne Place, and it introduced the "& Son" for the first time. The Westgate Hotel, 49 Cowbridge Road, and 49 Westbourne Place were the same address, as at that time Cowbridge Road between Lower Cathedral Road and Green Street was known as Westbourne Place.

Frederick, whom it is assumed was the 'son' in "& Son" would have been fourteen years old in September 1891, and his younger brother William would have been ten, and both were still at school. It is surprising perhaps that Joseph chose "& Son" rather than use the plural, unless this is once more a deliberate omission, or William is again considered to be too young.

Up to this point the mineral water firm had been in the name of H. F. Smallcombe, which indicates that possibly J. Smallcombe and Son is the wine and spirit merchanting business, which is separate from the mineral water manufacturing business. Perhaps this was calculated to separate the alcoholic from the non-alcoholic side of the business. It is also the first and only mention of a factory at Saltmead, although the name Saltmead appears printed on the side of Joseph's earthenware ginger beer bottles. A local map showing a survey date of 1876-8, revised in 1899 shows the area around Saltmead Road, to be called Saltmead, with Allerton Street being two streets along from Saltmead Road, so in all probability Joseph was referring to Allerton Street when he indicated a factory in Saltmead. The area known as Saltmead included the area now bordered by the railway tracks and Leckworth Industrial Estate, and all became part of Grangetown. The housing in this area was built on the Windsor Estate land and mainly comprised streets of working class terraced houses, without front gardens. It is unlikely that Joseph owned the freehold of any of his properties, as ninety percent of all houses in

Cardiff at this time were tenanted, but he could have purchased the ninety-nine year lease.

It is known that Sevenoaks Park, less than half a mile from Allerton Street, was locally known as the Tan, or Pop Alley Park, as it was said that there used to be a Pop Factory on the site of the park. This might well have been the site of the mineral water manufacturer South Wales Aerated Water Company that operated from Penarth Road.

At this time public transport was also expanding, and by 1892 tramways went from Roath to the Docks, from Canton to the Docks, from St. John's Square to Canton, and from Clifton Street to Grangetown, together with ten listed bus routes.

On Friday the 1st April 1892 Joseph and Harriet were presented with their first granddaughter, Harriet Hornblow. Harriet was born at 46 Clare Road, St. Mary, Cardiff, to the west of the docks, about three quarters of a mile west of Adam Street, and now part of the Clare Court Hotel. Her father William, who registered the birth, was listed as a Hotel barman. Although nobody at 46 Clare Road was listed in the 1891/2 Electoral Roll it is probable that the family lived there between the times that Joseph relinquished his licence in August 1891, and when he re-appeared at 32 Clare Road in May 1893. This possibility is reinforced by the fact that Joseph's daughter Rhoda records this as her address when she married in July 1892.

The joy of the family was to be short-lived, however, as the infant Harriet, having been born prematurely, died nineteen days later on Tuesday the 19th April, whilst still at 46 Clare Road. Her father William registered the death the following day.

Three months later Joseph and Harriet had the expense of another wedding when Harriet Hannah's younger sister, who is now recorded as Rhoda Rose, and is seventeen years old, married Samuel Ernest Venning Weeks, a confectioner of 40 Augusta Street. They married at the Zion Baptist Chapel, Longcross Street, Cardiff, on Sunday the 17th July 1892, and perhaps it was one of those fairy tale weddings, of childhood sweethearts. When Rhoda was growing up at numbers 65 and 88 Adam Street, Samuel's grandparents were living at number 40 Adam Street. Although Samuel was five or six years older than Rhoda their paths might frequently have crossed when Samuel visited his grandparents whilst the families lived in the same street over a period of some 6 years or so. When Joseph's family moved out of Adam Street, Rhoda would have been ten years old, but, as we have seen, the family moved within a very small geographical area.

Zion Baptist Chapel, Longcross Street

On the marriage certificate Rhoda increases her age by one year to eighteen, and Samuel reduces his by one year to twenty-four. Joseph, who is still listed as a wine and spirit merchant, was a witness together with his wife Harriet, as Samuel's father was dead by this time. This area was all very local to Rhoda as Augusta Street was one street north of Eclipse Street, and Longcross Street was two streets further north. Rhoda gave her address as 46 Clare Road.

On the first of May 1893, William Hornblow, still a barman, and Harriet presented Joseph and Harriet with a second grandchild, a son William Lionel, at 32 Clare Road, Grange, Cardiff. As will be seen later William Lionel did survive, unlike his deceased sister Harriet.

On the 8th October 1893 Joseph and Harriet were presented with another grandson, this time by daughter Rose, who registered the birth, and son-in-law Ernest Weeks, both of whom used their second names rather than Rhoda and Samuel. Samuel had now progressed to a journeyman baker, which means that he had finished his training or apprenticeship and was now a qualified baker. The child, Rose and Ernest's first, was named Ernest Douglas Smallcombe Weeks, and he

44

was born in Llandaff, Cardiff, almost certainly at Imperial Buildings, off the High Street, near Mary Street.

Joseph and Harriet lived at 32 Clare Road from 1893 to 1894, which later becomes a Stationers and tobacconists, and later still a greengrocers. Joseph then moves into the same address as the HFS business at 67 Clare Road in 1894-5, for one year. Sixty-seven Clare Road was listed as a business address for HFS from 1894 to 1897, later to become a hairdresser's shop, and it would appear that at this time William and Harriet Hornblow set up home independent of Joseph and Harriet.

The whole family would now be aware that Cardiff was still developing in all directions, and there were many business opportunities, leisure attractions and amusements for the Victorians of all classes to enjoy. The Music Halls were by now respectable after many years as a disreputable form of entertainment, and there was a big rise in amateur dramatics and a boom in such luxury goods as ice cream, fish and chips, and cigarettes.

Possibly Joseph and Harriet, with some of the children and perhaps grandchildren, might have walked the mile and a half from Clare Road to see the opening of the grand Roath Park on the 20th June 1894. The one hundred acre park, narrow but about a mile long, with its boating lake, paddling pool, bandstand, and gardens, would have been a welcome distraction from the busy life of a minor Cardiff entrepreneur.

This picture shows the popularity of Roath Park in Edwardian times.

At their new home at 35 Clare Road, Grange, Cardiff, on the 29th December 1894, William and Harriet Hornblow were blessed with another daughter, Gladys Constance, who was Joseph and Harriet's fourth grandchild, their second granddaughter. William Hornblow had now progressed from a barman to a Licensed Victualler, as had his father-in-law Joseph before him.

Rose, once more recorded as Rose Rhoda, and Samuel Ernest Venning Weeks who registered the birth and listed his full name, produced their second child, Joseph and Harriet's fifth grandchild, Daisy Constance, on Tuesday the 6th August 1895, whilst still living in the Imperial Buildings, Llandaff. Ernest, as he was known, was now shown to be a 'Baker master', and he was working from 70 Conway Road, Canton. This would have been a new shop at the time, as in the previous year's Directory the numbers in Conway Road only reach 50 on the even side and 87 on the odd side.

In 1896 HFS was listed under the residential section at 36 Clare Road, and F.W. Smallcombe is also listed at this address, which was Harriet Hornblow (Senior)'s house in 1889. This has to be considered to be, not an unusual, misprint or misreporting, as there was no F. W. Smallcombe in Cardiff at that time. Whether this was Frederick Joseph, William Albert, or Frederick and William there is no way of knowing, but Harriet Hornblow is recorded at that address from 1897 to 1902. Joseph and Harriet then appeared listed in the residential section under HFS at 38 Clare Road in 1897, where they stayed until 1914.

HFS is shown in Allerton Street under the Directory's Business section as 'Stores' from 1894-1896, and the HFS business is also shown under the number 14 Allerton Street in 1897. Harriet Hornblow (Senior) reappears at 36 Clare Road in 1897.

Also in 1897, on Wednesday the 3rd March at 1 George Street, Blaenavon, Dorothy May Weeks was born to Rhoda, as she styled herself, and Samuel Ernest Venning Weeks, now curiously returned to a journeyman baker. It appears that Ernest and Rhoda must have moved from Llandaff to Blaenavon in 1896, but the reason for the move is unclear, particularly bearing in mind the newness of the shop in Conway Road. This is the first time we find any members of the family outside the confines of Cardiff, and one has to wonder if Ernest was unable to make it on his own, and decided to move away

46

from the area where he was a self-employed baker-master, to work for another baker as an employee. Dorothy was destined to remain unmarried, become a seamstress by trade, and live to the ripe old age of one hundred and two.

On the 22nd of June 1897 the nation celebrated the Diamond Jubilee of Queen Victoria, 60 years on the throne, and the only Monarch under whom most of the population had lived. Apart from the official celebrations, street parties were held in every parish, and all the Queen's subjects enjoyed a national holiday.

The seventh, and last, grandchild of the nineteenth century for Joseph and Harriet was Frederick Joseph Hornblow, the second son of Harriet and William, born at 36 Clare Road, Grange, Cardiff, on the 21st August 1898. William is now shown to be a 'spirits vaults cellar-man'. It looks as if the baby was named after his uncle Frederick Joseph Smallcombe, whose twenty-first birthday was the following month.

After Fred's twenty-first birthday on the 23rd of September 1898, the family appear to have had a less eventful period until the New Year of 1900, although, for some reason, Joseph took out a mortgage on the Allerton Street property on the 1st of May 1899, which he redeemed in October 1913.

On the international scene the newspapers of the day would be full of the Boer War, which had been brewing for some years between the Dutch descended Afrikaners, or Boers, and the British Settlers in South Africa, who had spread from the original colony on the Cape of Good Hope. War was declared on October 12th 1899 and lasted for two and a half years, during which time the sieges of Ladysmith, and Mafeking in particular, found their way into history.

# Chapter Five

## Joseph's Mineral Water Manufacturing Business

There can be little doubt that Joseph was the proprietor of the mineral water manufacturing business although the first impression is that the ownership of the business is confused. The mineral water manufacturing business was first referred to in the Western Mail Cardiff Directory in 1889 and is first mentioned in Kelly's Directory in 1895, and subsequent Directories. The business was listed in the name of Joseph's wife Harriet, and Joseph did not describe himself as a mineral water manufacturer until 1900. The business was then listed in the name of Joseph in the 1906 and 1910 Kelly's Directories.

There is possibly a simple explanation for this apparent anomaly. Joseph was the licensee of the Westgate Hotel from 1885 to 1891. He was a wine and spirit merchant from 1891 to 1900. Perhaps he would have felt that it was improper to start a business in 1894 with "Temperance" in the business title under such circumstances, or perhaps felt that there were enough business enterprises in his name at that time. Joseph appears to have left the wine and spirit business about 1900, and this is possibly why the mineral water business was recorded in his name by 1906.

It is perhaps appropriate at this stage to describe exactly what it was that Joseph and the family did as aerated mineral water manufacturers, but before considering the process itself, perhaps we should consider the logistics of setting up such an operation. In terms of space the requirement would not be great, initially. A small pilot scheme could have been housed in a room about fifteen feet square, perhaps in the Westgate Hotel, in which, apart from the manufacturing equipment it would be possible to stack two hundred dozen clean bottles with outside storage for the same number of empties awaiting cleaning. These conditions would be cramped and as turnover increased it would be necessary to expand the space required.

The cost of setting up the operation is not quite so easy to judge, as it means comparing the prices of the day with current prices, and there are such a large variety of factors to consider that comparisons are not easy. The wage level required to satisfy a family one hundred years ago would be judged by the cost of providing necessaries. The modern idea of necessaries is completely different to that of the nineteenth century. The extent of credit facilities, the proliferation of luxury goods, holidays as we know them, or even a five day week was not a part of the world of the nineteenth century worker, and walking five miles to work six days a week would not cause surprise. Income tax was a fraction of present levels, and body and soul could be kept together, and usually had to be, on much smaller wages pro rata than by the modern worker. If we use a very rough rule of thumb and suggest that a modern pound (in the year 2000) would purchase fifty pounds worth of goods in 1900, this would be fair as far as general goods were concerned. It must be emphasised that this figure is of little use in comparing items 'across the board'. For example a house bought in 1900 would now cost several hundred times that figure. Even a comparatively low paid worker can in modern times afford a car, whereas the Victorian worker could only dream of owning his own carriage. To assess the cost of initially setting up in business it is necessary to examine exactly what would have been Joseph's requirements, and the availability of the means of production.

It is probable that Joseph set up the mineral water manufacturing business to supply his own needs at the Westgate Hotel, then expanded it with his wine and spirit merchanting business, giving him a ready made outlet. We know that Joseph used glass Codd's bottles for his aerated mineral water, which were bottles with a crimped neck containing a glass marble. These bottles were invented in 1875, and were widely used by 1885, but earthenware bottles were used for ginger beer. Bratby and Hinchliffe of London and Manchester advertised their bottles in The Mineral Water Trade Review and Guardian Supplement, at seventeen and sixpence a gross, but Joseph bought his from Barnard of London, and clearly bought sufficient quantities to have SMALLCOMBE CARDIFF embossed on the side and, H.S. embossed on the bottom.

The ginger beer bottle on the left is overprinted with H.F. Smallcombe & Co –
Cardiff- Saltmead Works. The Codd's bottle on the right is embossed H.S.
on the Base, and Smallcombe, Cardiff on the sides.

Note: The author has in his possession several of Joseph's Codd's bottles, patented
by Hiram Codd, in green glass in 1871. William Barnard, the manufacturer, existed
from 1863 at Paul's Wharf, 24 Upper Thames Street, London, and moved to 54
Crutched Friars in 1875, then to King William Street in 1885. In 1897 the firm
became William Barnard and Sons, Bottle Manufacturers, and moved to 66
Fenchurch Street until 1930 when the firm moved to 10 Lloyds Avenue, where it
remained until it closed in 1966.

As a modern update to the story of Joseph's mineral water factory at 12
Allerton Street, in August 1999 a Mr. Squires retired from these same premises,
having used them as a builder's yard for thirty years. When he first moved into the
premises he cleared out a load of 'pop' bottles and pickle jars. Prior to the
occupation by Mr. Squires the yard had also been used as a builder's yard. The
premises consist in a substantial yard, and a two storey building one hundred and
thirty six feet long and twenty-four feet deep, which at one time had planning
permission for a block of six flats.

The first step in the manufacturing process was to prepare the weekly mix of flavourings, colourings and spices. A spice grinder was used for powdering the spices such as ginger, and the essences such as orange, raspberry, lemon and lime, would have been mixed to specific recipes, and carefully decanted.

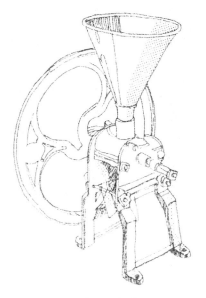

A spice grinder

The syrup, or twaddle, was mixed from sugar, saccharin, tartaric acid and water, the flavourings were then added and the mixture stored in a closed vat.

It appears to be the case that this process might have led to two modern derogatory phrases. It is said that beer drinkers used to refer disparagingly to those who drank lemonade as Codd's wallopers, cod's wallop now being a slang term for nonsense; and perhaps the same author coined another phrase related to the syrup used in the process that was called 'twaddle'. A load of old twaddle would have been useless if unused at the end of the week.

The carbon dioxide gas for the 'fizz' was manufactured on the premises by mixing powdered chalk, with dilute sulphuric acid in a wooden barrel. The gas was then stored in a small gasholder, until it was injected with the liquid into the bottle.

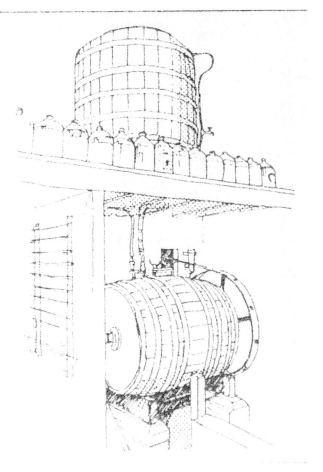

A simple inexpensive gas plant. More sophisticated machinery was
on sale by specialist manufacturers, but would be more costly.

The Codd's bottle filling was a simple hand operated process,
which at the time Joseph first started only filled one bottle at a time.
The bottle was inverted on an upright stand, and a wire mesh guard
protected the operator as the bottle was filled under pressure with
water, carbon dioxide, and syrup. The bottle was then righted and the
pressure of the gas kept the marble tight against a seal in the rim.

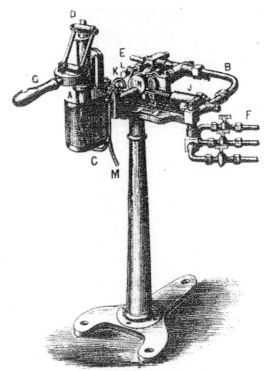

Patent Turnover Bottling Machine.

To release the bottle's stopper it was necessary to use a Codd's bottle opener that was placed on the top of the bottle and banged down, releasing the gas pressure allowing the glass marble to drop back to the base of the neck. The bottle was then held with the two crimps downwards, allowing the marble to become trapped, and thereby allowing the free flow of mineral water from the bottle.

During the manufacturing process bottles were known to explode under pressure, but took only two to three seconds to fill. Theoretically this meant that one operator could easily fill ten thousand bottles in a twelve-hour hour shift. There were, however, probably four limiting factors. Firstly, accumulating the bottles for the operator to fill, secondly the dispersal of filled bottles, thirdly the supply of bottles from the washing process, and fourthly the sale and delivery of ten thousand bottles a day.

The washing and removal of old labels was a considerable operation in itself. The bottles were washed in a wooden vat after being rotated on a wheel device used for soaking and removing the labels. Needless to say the whole cleaning process was a messy protracted business, certainly the bottles could not be de-labelled and washed at the same speed that an operator could fill them.

Bottle Soaking
Wheel
Used for soaking
paper labels from
bottles prior to
refilling.

Trying to picture the operation as Joseph and his family might have carried it out requires an assessment of the family situation as a whole. In August 1891 Joseph relinquished the licence of the Westgate Hotel, presumably to concentrate on the business of wine and spirit merchant. By 1895 there was Joseph, Harriet, and Frederick, now eighteen, with Rhoda Rose and Harriet Hannah now married, and William aged fourteen about to leave school. So, there were effectively only three members of the family available to work at the manufacturing process on a full time basis. Once the business was working the three members could spend one day preparing bottles, cleaning and de-labelling. One day could be spent collecting orders, invoicing, and preparing the mixtures and gas. In one day one

54

of the three could supply the bottles to the machine operator, one fill the bottles and one remove the bottles from the work area and crate them ready for delivery. Joseph's son Frederick probably did the delivery work, and is probably the person shown in a photograph of a man outside a pub in Cardiff with his horse and cart sign written Smallcombe of Cardiff.

The Smallcombe delivery cart outside the Railway Hotel, Llandaff

There would still have been time in the working week for other business enterprises, and an expansion of the mineral water business once both boys had left school, or the development of the delivery side of the business into a haulage firm.

Joseph would have had little difficulty in purchasing second hand machinery in the 1890s, and could have found such machinery advertised in the trade journal referred to earlier. In 1886 Wilcocks advertised a New Registered Design and Patent machine for filling several different types of internal stoppered bottles, including Codd's and Vallet Bottles. The machine weighed one hundred and thirty pounds and cost seven pounds ten-shillings new, but Bratby and Hinchliffe claimed that their machine was better and faster at ten pounds.

# WILCOCKS'

## New Registered Design and Patent

### APPLIED TO

# TURNOVER | FILLING | MACHINE,

### For Filling Internal Stopper Bottles.

Syrup Pump
empties
itself every Stroke.

Can be seen

at work

at

**BACK STREET,**

**BATH.**

THIS NEW FILLING
MACHINE is an immense
improvement on any hither-
to introduced to the Bottling
Trade, having fewer work-
ing parts, and is the most simple and
quickest Bottle Filler of any. The
atmospheric air is more effectually expelled from the bottles in filling than
in any other Turnover; the automatic
arrangement for settling of syrup is perfection;
the regulation of the syrup is done in an
instant by a thumb-screw above, from
the smallest quantity to three ounces;
this thumb-screw puts the Syrup Pump
in or out of work as desired; the working parts and valves are outside, and
can be got at in a moment; the action
is a rotary motion in one direction;
the action for righting the stopper is
unique, and does not interfere with the
Syrup Pump. This Machine is a great
Saver of Syrup.

Total Weight, 130 lbs.

*VERY STRONG IN EVERY PART, AND WELL FINISHED.*

This Filling Machine was at work at our Stand, No. 1 Bay, Agricultural Hall, National Exhibition and Market, in October last, and is quite a success. A large number have been supplied and are universally liked. It fills Codd's Bottles, as well as others, to perfection. We have a continuous run of orders.

COMPLETE, as Engraving, with Glass Barrel Syrup Pump, } **£7 : 10 : 0**

The machine was an upright stand with the working parts at a convenient height. The machine dispensed the syrup from a pump, which was capable of delivering any quantity up to three ounces at a time, and the manufacturers emphasised the point that the syrup pump emptied itself at every stroke. The machine filled the bottle with water in an inverted position, injected the syrup and gas, which expelled the air and then rotated the bottle. In the same trade journal Rylands also advertised their new machine, "The Rapid Paragon Turnover Filling Machine". The manufacturer claimed that this machine was the simplest on the market and would fill sixty to eighty dozen bottles an hour, which is one every five seconds. Great importance was obviously attached to the syrup pump, and Rylands claimed that theirs was the most reliable. The advertisement emphasised the simplicity of non-skilled repairs, and the fact that 'saves more gas, while allowing the air to escape more perfectly, than any other machine'. In contrast to the previous advertisement Rylands specifically points out that the syrup pump "does not empty itself at every stroke; should be sorry if it did". It claimed that there was no waste of water, no waste of gas, and no waste of syrup.

Rylands also advertised 'The Chemist's Plant' for making the gas. The plant to make "100 to 150 dozens per day" was thirty-five pounds, and the machines rose in size and price to one hundred and seventy five pounds for a machine to produce three thousand dozens per day. The machine comprised two parts standing side by side.

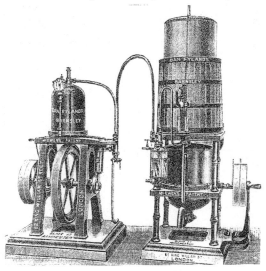

The Rylands Chemist Plant.

Bratby and Hinchliffe, however, produced an Anti-Atmospheric Generator and Gas Regulator that was a gasholder and generator combined. This would be more suitable in a confined space. The machine had a charging hopper on one side and an acid box on the other side fitted with an automatic acid feed valve which regulated the flow of acid onto the whiting, which was powdered chalk. The acid and chalk combined in the generator and the gas produced was stored in the gas regulator above, which was connected to the bottle-filling pump.

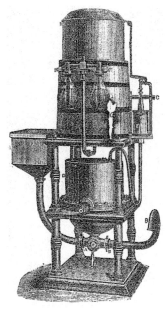

The Bratby & Hinchliffe anti-atmospheric generator
and gas regulator.

One of the claims made by most of these machinery manufacturers was that they were all hand operated, needed no steam, and "a boy or girl can fill easily 70 dozens an hour". Dows, Clark & Co made a different form of filler, operated by foot, which it claimed saved breakages of bottles to the extent that the cost of the machine could be recovered in one season. As the smallest Dows filler for four hundred dozens a day cost forty pounds, and the cost of bottles was seventeen and sixpence a gross this means that the manufacturer could expect twenty broken bottles a day, this could obviously cause considerable problems although it was less than one half percent. The Dows generating and bottling cylinders were set horizontally, and Hayward Tyler used yet a different formation, so Joseph would have been able to shop around for the configuration which best suited his available space. Hayward Tyler of London also bought sold and exchanged machinery, and new and second-hand machinery was also available from Bowlers of Bath.

Eventually the machinery became more automated, but even by 1912 the Riley "Vauxhall" automatic bottling machine, shown below, was only capable of seventy dozens an hour. The machine filled two bottles at a time had a base less than two feet square, was six feet tall and cost only twenty five pounds.

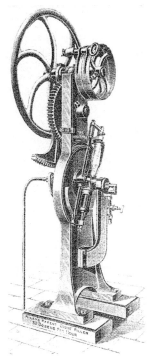

By the 1920s Barnett and Foster had developed a power operated "Gas Saver" Back-pressure Turnover Filling Machine capable of filling five bottles at a time at a rate of one hundred and forty dozen an hour, at a cost of one hundred and thirty two pounds, including the syrup pump. It is interesting to note that the Barnett and Foster advertisement refers to the fact that

"Clients have told us that on an average the operator may miss one in every twenty-four bottles, which, reckoned on the low basis of 11/2 oz. of syrup to each 10 oz. bottle, means a wastage of nearly 61/2 gals of syrup per working day. If syrup costs only 3/- a gallon, the perfect automatic cut-off effects a saving of 19/6d per working day in syrup alone, without calculating the cost of the aerated water that would otherwise be wasted."

This explains the continued emphasis on the quality of the syrup pumps over the years.

To put all of this into the context of the year 2000 we can roughly equate the cost of setting up a small factory. Joseph would have needed a filling machine, a gas plant, say four hundred dozens bottles, a washing trough, cordials, flavourings etc. The major capital outlay would be the machinery at say forty five pounds new, perhaps thirty pounds second hand, and four hundred dozen bottles would have cost about thirty pounds. The total outlay if using second hand machinery, including sundry items is likely to be about sixty-five pounds. In modern terms this would be probably around three to four thousand pounds. If one looks at the machinery in modern terms this would not seem an unreasonable price, and for a man who to better himself had saved wisely, this would seem to be within his reach.

There was, however, local competition in the mineral water manufacturing business at that time. Basher and Son worked from Eldon Street from 1887 to 1889; Anthony Birrell, Pearce and Co., was at 59 and 61 Clare Road in 1889 and 1900; and F.W. Smart at 53 Clare Road from 1892 to 1897. The South Wales Aerated Water Company operated from Penarth Road in 1900; W.R. Harding & Co., were at 61 Clare Road from 1901 to 1905, and at 59 Clare Road from 1903 to 1905. The Northern Bottling Co., were established at 37 Saltmead Street from 1894 to 1910, although they appear to have been taken over by John Archer in 1906.

Having said that Joseph had a ready-made market within the family. His daughter Harriet Hannah married William Hornblow in 1891, and at that time William's brother John T. Hornblow, aged 24 was at the Five Bells, 19 Cristina Street, which ran parallel to Bute Street, in the middle of the docks, and by 1894 William himself had become a licensed victualler.

Although there is no known connection, it is perhaps a coincidence that the first named opposition, Basher & Son, has the same name as one of the witnesses at Joseph's wedding, Alfred William Basher.

# Chapter Six
## Joseph and his family move into the Twentieth Century
### 1900 - 1913

The family moved into the 20th Century with the marriage of their daughter Beatrice, aged twenty-one, to Henry Washbourne, aged twenty four, on Sunday the 25th March 1900. On the marriage certificate Henry was recorded as a farmer living at Tower Hill in Bristol, which was an address in the centre of the City, near Castle Green. Beatrice gave her address as Jacob Street Bristol, which was a turning off Tower Hill. Beatrice's sister Harriet Hornblow was one of her witnesses, and there were two others, Edwin Collins, presumably Henry's best man, and Evelyn Norris, probably a bridesmaid, neither of who appear in subsequent records. For the first time at one of his daughter's weddings Joseph was not a witness, but he was described as a mineral water manufacturer, and the Smallcombe family still lived at 38 Clare Road, and were still using the Allerton Street store. As there is no occupation for Beatrice on the marriage certificate it has to be presumed that she was not in service or working, so her address at Jacob Street was probably an accommodation address for the purposes of the banns. Possibly Henry had got a job working on a farm about 1893, at the age of seventeen, when his parents moved from Clay Lane into the Codrington Arms.

The Codrington Arms.

61

One obvious question to arise from this marriage was. "How did Beatrice and Henry meet?" The answer might give an interesting insight into the Smallcombe family life at the time. It will be recalled that there is a lasting query as to how much interaction, if any, there was between Joseph and his mother and his siblings. The same question would apply to Joseph's wife Harriet and her family in Iron Acton. The 1881 Census shows that Harriet's parents George and Mary Dyer were still living in Clay Lane, Iron Acton. In the 1851 Census George, Harriet's father, had been a coal miner, but by the time of the 1881 Census he had become an agricultural labourer. Harriet's brother George had married, and was still living in the area at Engine Common, Yate, but Harriet's eldest brother James does not appear on the 1881 Census.

This leaves Harriet's brother Pharaoh, whom we know to have been living and working in Cardiff with his wife Mary, and their extensive family. The 1881 Census shows that Pharaoh's sister-in-law Kate Drinkwater, a nineteen-year-old general servant, was with them at the time of the Census, and as Pharaoh's wife Mary and her sister Kate were born in Wickwar, it is reasonably certain that Mary Dyer was the daughter of William Drinkwater, a cordwainer in Wickwar High Street, and his wife Annis.

From this information it looks as if there was probably a current connection between Harriet and Pharaoh in Cardiff and the Dyer and Drinkwater families in Iron Acton and Wickwar. This is compounded by the fact that Henry Washbourne, aged five at the 1881 Census, is found with his family, father John and mother Christina, living in Clay Lane, Iron Acton only a few doors away from Beatrice's grandparents, the Dyer family. It can be safely assumed that Beatrice met her future husband Henry Washbourne on visits with her mother or uncle Pharaoh, to see Harriet's parents in Clay Lane Iron Acton.

At the 1891 Census the fifteen year old Henry Washbourne, usually known as Harry, is still at home at Clay Lane, Iron Acton with his parents John and Christanna (sic), and two brothers, William aged twenty-six, and James aged twenty, sister Jane aged nineteen, and a young female relative, Evlin A. Washbourne, born in Wickwar. Robert Washbourne, now twenty-nine years of age, is no longer at home. In the Census John Washbourne was listed as an Engine

Driver. From 1893 to 1898 John is listed in the Bristol Directory as living at the Codrington Arms, Iron Acton, but on Henry and Beatrice's marriage certificate in 1900 John is recorded as an Engineer. Moving ahead for a moment, the records of 1903 show John Washbourne's son, Robert, occupying a freehold beer house with no name, at Yate, the freehold being owned by his father John. John Washbourne is the occupier of the Codrington Arms, an alehouse at Iron Acton, owned by Arnold Perett, brewers. By 1906 Robert is listed as a beer retailer at the Cross Roads, Yate, and John's establishment is listed as the Codrington Arms, a Public House.

Returning to 1900, it should be remembered that later in the year, that is, on the 1st November 1900, Joseph reached his half-century, and five weeks later Henry and Beatrice produced Joseph and Harriet's eighth grandchild, their fifth granddaughter. Williamina Beatrice was born on the eighth of December 1900 at the Codrington Arms, Iron Acton, her father Henry, who registered the birth, was recorded as a farmer.

Back in Cardiff the records show that in 1901 J. Sperin, a furniture remover, occupied 12 Allerton Street and William Pearce, a carpenter, occupied number 14. Harriet Hornblow (Senior) was living at 34 Clare Road, and Joseph's family were still at 38 Clare Road, whilst still using the Allerton Street store.

Outside the immediate family environment this year had a very special significance. On January the 22nd the eighty-one year old Queen Victoria, who had reigned since she was eighteen years old, died at her home on the Isle of Wight. Joseph and a great many other British citizens had lived their entire lives under the one Monarch, and the historical Victorian period came to an end, to be succeeded by the 'Edwardian days'. One particularly patriotic event was instituted around this period, and that was Empire Day held on the second Monday in March, a day in which school children took flags to school, and parades were held to commemorate the assistance given to Britain by the Colonies during the Boer War.

In 1902 there occurred the next major event in the story of the Smallcombe family. Joseph and Harriet's ninth grandchild, Harriet Sarah Washbourne, was born at the Codrington Arms to Beatrice and Harry on the 4th of December. Harry, using his formal name of Henry, again registered the birth, and was still recorded as a farmer.

Back in Cardiff Joseph and his family might have taken a day off from work to celebrate, and to see the first electric tram that had been introduced into the city that year, a sight not available in the quiet rural surrounding of Beatrice's new Gloucestershire home.

A 1902 Electric Tram

Unfortunately, Joseph and Harriet's delight at the birth of their sixth granddaughter must have been severely muted by the serious condition of their youngest surviving daughter. Yet again Joseph and Harriet were to lose another child in the tragic death of their nineteen-year-old daughter Florence Blanche, who died of tuberculosis on Saturday the 27th December 1902, at 38 Clare Road, Grangetown, Cardiff. One can imagine the distraught Christmas in the Smallcombe household that year, the first disrupted Christmas since the birth of Lily Ada seventeen years earlier. Joseph, still occupied as a mineral water manufacturer, was present at his daughter's death, and he registered it on Monday the 29th December. For the third time Hannah and Joseph buried their currently youngest daughter, and the family made the journey to the grave in which

64

rested Lily Ada and Alice Maud. Florence Blanche was buried with her two sisters at three o'clock on New Years' Eve, Wednesday 31st December. Again Mr. Marsh made the arrangements.

This death indicates that the family were still living in Clare Road, but other records indicate that in 1902 the family moved to 12 Allerton Street, whilst also retaining the premises at 38 Clare Road. It is probable that the family initially used part of the store behind 12 Allerton Street as business premises, and then moved in completely a little later, and it is probable that Joseph and Harriet's son, William Albert, carried on his haulage business behind the premises of 14 and 12 Allerton Street, beside which there was an alleyway allowing access to the yard which had a two storey building at the rear. Between 1902 and 1911 the premises at number 12 were shared with Mrs. Elizabeth Allen according to the Business section of the Western Mail Cardiff Directory. There is no reference to Mrs. Allen at number 12 Allerton Street in the residential section of the Directory, so it is possible that it was only a business arrangement.

By 1903 Joseph and Harriet's daughter Harriet Hannah and her husband William Hornblow were licensees of the Locomotive Inn at 296 Bute Street.

William and Harriet Hannah, with William Lionel, Gladys and Frederick Joseph.
Probably taken about 1902-3

Also in 1903 there is an address that appears to claim another family connection. It will be recalled that Joseph's brother-in-law, Pharaoh Dyer, was working as a blacksmith at 107 and 103 Castle Road up to 1883. By 1893 Pharaoh was listed as a 'wheelwright' at 119 Castle Road, Roath, and more significantly by 1905 as a blacksmith and carriage builder at that same address. Pharaoh appears to have moved at some point to a larger house at 183 City Road sometime around 1908. (To avoid confusion it should be pointed out that the name Castle Road was changed to City Road before 1908, although the Directories for 1908 to 1915 still showed addresses as "Castle Road, now City Road", and indeed the name plate for Castle Road was still standing alongside the City Road name plate as late as the 1950s). The listing of Pharaoh as smith and wheelwright continued until 1918 at both 119 City Road, and his home address of 183 City Road, and although Pharaoh died in 1919 his wife Mary stayed on at 183 City Road. The firm of P. Dyer and Son continued at 119 City Road, as carriage builders, farriers, and blacksmiths until the end of the 1920s, and by 1932 was listed as G. Dyer and Sons carriage builders and farriers, this would be George Dyer, Pharaoh's son, who in 1926 was shown to be living at 183 City Road. It would appear that during the 1930s, George Dyer, Harriet Smallcombe's nephew, leased the premises at 119 City Road to Frederick Joseph Hornblow, Harriet and Joseph's grandson. The evidence for this is a family anecdote to this effect, and the fact that Frederick Joseph Hornblow at some time during the 1930s had a car sales business at 29/31 City Road, "previously at 119". Frederick Joseph Hornblow certainly rented the premises from George Dyer as late as the Second World War in 1939.

TELEPHONE 26454

## ROATH MOTOR COMPANY

THE

 USED CAR SPECIALISTS

SALES & SERVICE

AGENTS FOR ALL PRINCIPAL MAKES

29/31 CITY ROAD, CARDIFF

PREVIOUSLY No 119

Little is known of the family for a while, but in October 1905 there were celebrations in Cardiff when it was presented with its

66

Royal Charter, and became a City. The year 1907, however, saw the birth of the last of Joseph and Harriet's grandchildren, and their fourth grandson. Henry George Joseph John Washbourne was born at the Codrington Arms on the eighteenth of February 1907, to Harry and Beatrice. Again Harry (Henry) as a farmer registered the birth.

This 1906 horse bus was not confined to tram lines as was the horse tram.

It is not inappropriate at this time to contemplate one of the continuing mysteries of Joseph's life, and perhaps one of the tragedies of Joseph's tale. Joseph's mother, now Hannah Dunkerley, died in Scarborough on the eighteenth of February 1912, but it is not known whether or not there was any contact between Joseph and his mother, or Joseph and his siblings after he left the workhouse. The chronology of the two branches of the family since Joseph and Harriet left Bristol in 1872 or 1873 yields no clues, but we know that Joseph's mother, Hannah, moved to Scarborough between April 1871 and March1875. In 1871 Joseph's sister Mary Ann, was aged 13 living as a general servant on a farm in Pucklechurch. In June 1874 she was admitted to Bristol Infirmary, and she was admitted to the Chipping Sodbury workhouse in October 1875. Her whereabouts between June 1874 and October 1875 are a mystery, but Mary Ann appears with her mother in Scarborough by the time of the Census of 1881. Joseph's other sister, the 17 year old Georgina, was working in Bristol in 1881, and was married and living in Plymouth in March 1894. In March 1875 Joseph was labouring in Cardiff, by 1881 he was a barman, and by 1891 he was in business on his own account. There was only a short period of time between Joseph moving to

Cardiff and his mother moving to Scarborough, during which time Joseph was not particularly prosperous, and if there was any contact it might have occurred when members of Joseph's family visited the Dyer family in Iron Acton. It should also be borne in mind that during this early period Joseph and his family were constantly on the move. Georgina was in Bristol and Joseph would have to go to Bristol to get to Iron Acton, Mary Ann and Hannah were at Yate, and Joseph would have to go within 2 miles of Yate, or once the railways opened he would have to get out at Yate Station, which was the nearest stop to Iron Acton. Alas there are no clues as to the likelihood of family contact between Cardiff and Scarborough.

Two months after Joseph's mother died, there was another national tragedy, the sinking of the Titanic on the 15th April 1912, with the loss of more than fifteen hundred lives. Joseph could not have realised that the news of the sinking of this 'unsinkable' ship would have such a lasting effect on the imagination of the western world.

By 1912 Joseph's daughter Harriet Hannah, and her husband William Hornblow, had left the Locomotive Inn, and moved to another public house, the Custom House Inn at 265 Bute Street. There is in existence a School Leaving Certificate for Frederick Joseph Hornblow, dated 1912 with the address given as the Custom House, so it appears that the family lived at the Custom House although they were listed in the local directories at 242 Cathedral Road from as early as 1905, until as late as 1913. Certainly Joseph and his son-in-law William had some characteristics in common, particularly the licensing trade, and the entrepreneurial spirit for branching out.

As mentioned earlier it was in October 1913 that Joseph redeemed the mortgage that he had taken out on the Allerton Street property, and in that same year William Hornblow appears as a taxicab proprietor with an address at 1a Ryder Street. At the time of writing, and probably in 1913, this address would appear to be a large lock-up garage. The most significant thing about this entry is that as with all Directories the information is processed the previous year, which means that William's taxicab business must have been running by 1912. No William Hornblow appears in the commercial directory, other than Harriet's William; the entries cease the year of William's death, and the Ryder Street lock-up was only a five-minute walk from William's home. Apart from all this, the 1881 Census only shows the one Hornblow family living in Cardiff, so there can be little doubt that this is Harriet's William. The earlier research into Joseph's hansom cab business revealed that in London the motor taxicab started to overtake the horse drawn cab about this time, but it was said that in the provinces the change over was much delayed. It would appear that William's taxi business certainly must have been a forerunner of provincial motorised taxicabs.

William could have bought this six-year-old second hand taxi cab for £100- £200 in 1912, or perhaps he could have been able to afford the new luxurious Lanchester shown below.

In fact the change over from horse drawn to motor taxicabs in Cardiff is very interesting, and it was necessary for any potential taxicab proprietor to get his sums correct before embarking on the venture. It is recorded that the cost of two horses, plus the harness, and a spare horse would cost about a hundred and seventy five pounds at this time, whereas a new motor taxicab would cost about three hundred and fifty pounds. Petrol cost eight-pence (three pence in decimal money) a gallon, that is less than a penny a litre, then there was oil and servicing of the vehicle, just as there was food, bedding and veterinary fees for the horse owner. Statutory cab fares are listed in the directories of the time for horse drawn cabs. In 1893 the fare had been one shilling for the first mile or part of a mile, and nine-pence per mile thereafter. In 1911 the same fare applied, but the directory also adds a fare for Motor Taxi Cabs for the first time, for one and up to four persons, any distance not exceeding half a mile, sixpence, and for each succeeding part of a mile a further tuppence (two pence). The fare tariff changes as time passes, but by 1922 the term 'Horse Drawn Cab' is used, as a distinction, but more significantly by 1928 the tariff for horse drawn cabs is no longer recorded. There is, however, in 1928, a rate for 'Motor Taxi Cycles' at sixpence for up to three quarters of a mile and tuppence per mile thereafter; these rates are still shown in the 1937 Directory.

# Chapter Seven

## The War Years
## 1914-1918

In the Western Mail Cardiff Directories for 1914 and 1915 Joseph is to be found in the local residents and street directory sections at 12 Allerton Street, listed as a mineral water manufacturer, but not listed anymore in the business section. It appears to be the case that the family moved out of 38 Clare Road in 1914.

During this period Joseph and his family were to see life starting to change drastically for everyone. The horse drawn tram and bus of ten years ago was being replaced by the electric tram and double-decker bus, the horse and cart was working alongside its petrol driven competitor, and the live theatres were being replaced by the silent cinemas, such as Cardiff's Splott Cinema which opened in 1913. Not only was transport and entertainment changing but so too was the 'art' of warfare, with the cavalry about to be replaced by tanks, and ground warfare being supplemented with the primitive aircraft of the Royal Flying Corps. Only eleven years earlier had the Wright brothers made the first sustained flight for twelve seconds, a distance of one hundred and twenty feet, at a height of ten feet. By 1908 Orville Wright had made the first flight in an aeroplane of longer than one hour, yet by 1911 mail planes were operating and aircraft in the 1914-18 war were to fly at twenty five thousand feet at a speed of one hundred and fifty-five miles an hour.

On the 4th August 1914 England joined the war against Germany and large numbers of young men volunteered to fight in the Great War. Frederick Joseph was thirty-seven at this time, and William Albert was thirty-four.

Soon after the war started the family suffered another premature death. Harriet Hornblow's husband William died on Thursday the 21st January 1915, at 20 Balaclava Road, Roath, from a diabetic coma; he was forty-six years old. William was recorded as a retired licensed victualler, and his father-in-law Joseph Smallcombe, of 12 Allerton Street, was 'in attendance', and registered the death, which might throw some doubts on later apocryphal stories of a family rift involving William. On the other hand Joseph might have been there merely to support his daughter, and grandchildren. It is, however, more probable that the family rift stories have been misinterpreted, and refer to the events concerning Harriet Hannah, as commented upon later.

20 Balaclava Road, a totally different type of house from the type Joseph and Harriet always lived in.

The family anecdotes concerning William's death refer in the main to the facts that Harriet had to put a jug full of water, from the then common bedroom jug and basin set used for washing, beside William's bed every night, and that William was said to go out frequently in his slippers because of his swollen feet. As William died in a diabetic coma, this makes perfect sense, and as Harriet and William had a horse and trap, the travelling in carpet slippers does not seem too eccentric.

The remaining family anecdote concerning William's death is much more interesting from the point of view of Joseph's story. It is said that after William died, Harriet had to sell all her possessions and then buy them back again, the main bone of contention being her piano. Research has shown that William did not leave a will, and that the Sureties for the Grant of Administration were Joseph Smallcombe of 12 Allerton Street his father-in-law, and Samuel Ernest Venning Weeks his sister-in-law's husband of 26 Wyndham Road. Under the laws of intestacy Harriet would retain all William's personal chattels, which would include all the household goods, which should include musical instruments, and even the family car, unless used for business purposes. If indeed Harriet had to sell her piano and then buy it back again, then Joseph and Samuel had made a mistake in understanding their obligations. William's estate amounted to nine hundred and eighty-eight pounds, sixteen-shillings and nine-pence gross, nine hundred and fifty-eight pounds, thirteen-shillings and ten-pence net, and was granted on the 22nd March 1915.

An important point arises as to Joseph's situation, from the documentation following the death of William. Samuel, as anticipated, is recorded as a baker, but Joseph is, for the first time recorded as a Pickle Manufacturer. This occupation for Joseph comes quite unexpectedly as there are no Directory references to Joseph as a Pickle Manufacturer, although there are family anecdotes from Yate, of pickles being sent from, or brought from, Cardiff. It was also said that Joseph manufactured his own vinegar. It has been noted, however, that after 1915 there are no further references to Joseph as a mineral water manufacturer.

On Monday the 25th January at twenty past two in the afternoon William was buried in a different section of Cathays Cemetery to which the Smallcombe family had been interred, in grave number V 225. In this case the Undertaker was Mr. A. J. Stone. It has to be said that there is something odd about the invoice for this burial. The invoice for the burials of Joseph and Harriet's three children are all the same, five-shillings interment, five-shillings digging, plus seven-shillings and four-pence for the Vicar, and four-shillings for the Sexton. The invoice for William's burial appears to have been originally five-shillings interment and eight-shillings and sixpence for digging, a total of thirteen-shillings and sixpence. A figure one has been placed in front of the five-shillings for interment, and eight-shillings and sixpence for digging crossed out and replaced by one pound two-shillings a sixpence, a total of one pound seventeen-shillings and sixpence, with ten-shillings for the Vicar and nothing for the Sexton. The strange thing is that three years later the next Smallcombe burial reverts to five-shillings for interment, and eight-shillings and sixpence for digging, with just five-shillings for the Vicar.

Joseph by now had reached what we currently call 'normal retiring age', that is sixty-five, on the 1st November 1915. In the Directories of 1915 and 1916 Joseph was listed as a resident at 12 Allerton Street, and there is no mention of his being a pickle or mineral water manufacturer, or being in any other form of business, so it appears that perhaps he had now retired.

Little is known about William Albert's haulage business but it is probable that it developed as an adjunct to the mineral water manufacturing business, with deliveries being made in the horse and cart, as can be seen in part of a contemporary photograph in Chapter Five from Stewart William's "Cardiff Yesterday No. 2."

Interestingly, the caption in the book refers to a delivery being made by H. F. Smallcombe. The driver sitting on the cart is not perfectly distinct, but certainly does not look like a man in his mid-sixties, so it was probably William Albert in his thirties. It is possible that if the mineral water business closed in 1915, then Frederick Joseph might have joined William in the haulage business, which could be borne out by the fact that Frederick Joseph is later referred to as a "Motor Driver". Clearly this would refer to an occupation rather than a mere skill, even in those early days, although it is of course possible that the motor Frederick Joseph drove might have been a taxicab.

Whatever Joseph's family situation was life became more concentrated on personal and domestic matters as the war with Germany progressed. On the 4th May 1916 the Government decreed that all men between eighteen and forty-one years of age were to be conscripted if the rate of volunteers fell below the required level. William Albert was at this time thirty-four, and Frederick Joseph was thirty-eight. William Albert was not conscripted, possibly he tried to enlist, but probably was rejected because of the bronchitis which eventually killed him a few years later. Frederick Joseph did however enlist in the Royal Engineers as a Sapper on Wednesday the 30th May 1917, where he became an engine driver.

Frederick Joseph Hornblow, the namesake of his uncle, and the nineteen-year-old son of Harriet Hannah was the first of Joseph and Harriet's grandchildren to marry. On Monday the 31st December 1917 he married Elsie Frances M. Griffiths, at the Cardiff Register Office. Frederick Joseph stated that he was a "2nd Air Mechanic", and twenty-one years old. His wife Elsie also stated that she was twenty-one, although she was in fact only seventeen. Frederick gave his address as Bute Docks, probably the barracks in Burt Street, and Elsie gave hers as the Philharmonic Hotel, Cardiff, both gave their parents' occupations as Licensed Victuallers. The witnesses at the marriage were J. R. Hyde and J. T. Lindsley.

The former Barracks at Burt Street, Bute Docks

It might be just a coincidence, but it might be remembered that the name of one of the witnesses at Joseph and Harriet's wedding, Basher, appeared again as a mineral water manufacturer in Cardiff, near where Joseph's firm operated. Strangely, at the wedding of Joseph and Harriet's grandson, the name of the other witness, Griffiths, was now duplicated.

In spite of the declaration on the marriage certificate of Frederick Joseph Hornblow, family legend has it that he was a dispatch rider. Perhaps this photograph confirms that fact, or was the cause of the family legend.

Frederick Joseph Smallcombe (not to be confused with Frederick Joseph Hornblow, his nephew) was discharged from the army on Thursday the 25th April 1918, nearly seven months before the end of the war, almost certainly on medical grounds. On Wednesday the 8th May 1918, less than two weeks after he was discharged from the army Frederick Joseph Smallcombe aged forty, died at 12 Allerton Street, of the tuberculosis from which he had been suffering for a year. His father Joseph was at home with Frederick when he died, and he registered the death on Saturday the 11th of May. It looks as if Frederick was suffering from TB before he enlisted, but one can imagine that the medical was not particularly thorough. The Great War ended with the Armistice in 1918 at the eleventh hour of the eleventh day of the eleventh month, although Sapper Smallcombe did not live to see the day. Once more Joseph and Harriet made the journey to grave L183 in Cathays Cemetery, this time for the burial of their fourth child. Frederick Joseph was buried with his three sisters at twenty past two in the afternoon of Tuesday the 14th May, with Mr. A.J. Stone making the arrangements. It is interesting to note that Frederick Joseph's death certificate shows him to be an "Ex-Sapper 287799 R.E. (Engine Driver)", but, as mentioned above, on his burial order he is recorded as a "Motor Driver". Presumably as Frederick only survived for two weeks after his discharge from the Army, and was probably very ill for sometime before, the reference to 'motor driver' applies to the period before he joined up in May 1917. A search has revealed that he did not leave a will.

Joseph and Harriet's grandson, William Lionel Hornblow, was the first of the family to make a permanent move away from the Wales - Gloucestershire area. On the ninth of April 1918 William married Caroline Conway at the Register Office at Paddington, in London. Both gave the address of 26 Star Street, which was a turning off the Edgware Road, half a mile or so from Paddington Main Line Station. William's occupation was recorded as a "1st Air Mechanic, Royal Flying Corps", he lists his father's occupation as being a Licensed Victualler, although his father had in fact been dead for over three years. This might indicate that William had been away from home since he was twenty-one, which would have been in 1914, and possibly that there might have been no communication with the family. This cannot be necessarily assumed to be true, as frequently the term 'Deceased' was omitted from parents' status on marriage certificates, but is borne out by a nephew who stated that he had met William Lionel at William's car showroom in the Edgware Road, London, and was sworn to secrecy as to his whereabouts. It is interesting, however, that the current family refer to William and his wife as Bill and Carrie. The witnesses at the marriage of William Lionel to Caroline were A. E. Stanley and H. Archer, Caroline's father William Conway was registered as a house painter. William Lionel's war record is certainly worth consideration for two very good reasons. Firstly, as in countless instances in this type of research, the dates do not make sense. William enlisted on the 5th March 1917, and gave his age as twenty-three years and eleven months. On the same sheet his date of birth is erroneously recorded as 5th April 1895. Had William been born on the 5th April 1895 then he would have been twenty one years and eleven months on the 5th March 1917, but his birth certificate shows that he was born on the 1st May 1893, which relates to neither date. If we take his twenty-three years and eleven months from his enlistment date of 5th March 1917, we return to 5th April 1893. It appears that William reduced his age by adding two years onto his year of birth, but gave his age in years and months correctly; but why did he choose the 5th April when his actual birth was the 1st May? In any event he could not have been born on the 5th April 1895, because that would only have been just over three months after the birth of his sister Gladys Constance on the 29th December 1894.

The second interesting thing about William's service is the historical aspect. He enlisted in the Royal Flying Corps branch of the Army on the 5th March 1917, and was transferred to the R.A.F. when it was formed by the amalgamation of the Royal Flying Corps and the Royal Navy Air Service on the 1st April 1918. William, service number 63862, was an air mechanic when he was married in April 1918, but was an assistant armourer by the time of his discharge, as being 'unfit', on the 25th January 1919. His service record shows him to have been five feet eleven and a half inches tall, a chest measurement of thirty-three inches, with fair hair, brown eyes and a fresh complexion. His address on discharge was still 26 Star Street Paddington, and he was shown to have been a film printer in civilian life. His record shows that his degree of proficiency was 'satisfactory', and he was awarded a Silver Star War Badge number 5741 on the 24th March 1919.

# Chapter 8

## Joseph and family
## 1918 - 1931

We now come to another of the little mysteries surrounding Joseph. We know that by 1918 his son Frederick Joseph was dead. It is suspected that Joseph's other son, William Albert, suffered from bronchitis, but probably still ran the haulage business, which he might have worked together with his late brother. In the Western Mail Cardiff Directories for 1918 to 1920 Joseph is still listed as a resident, but he is now referred to as a haulier, although he does not have an entry in the business section. It has to be possible that in 1918 Joseph, now sixty eight years of age, joined William in the haulage business in order to help out his ailing son, who must have suffered terribly during the winter months, out in all weathers with his bronchitis.

The year 1918 also saw Harriet, in common with most women over thirty years old, entitled to vote for the first time. By 1919 it appears that Joseph's widowed daughter Harriet Hannah had taken the licence of the Loudoun Hotel at 169-170 Bute Street, and by 1920 she was to move from there to the Bridge Hotel at 243-244 Bute Street. In fact the directories for 1920 show Harriet Hannah at the Loudoun Hotel, the Bridge Hotel, and 20 Balaclava Road, although this was the last entry at this address.

There are no further family records as the country recovered from the devastation of the Great War, until the beginning of 1920 when the family had a triple celebration. Firstly, on the 31st of January Frederick Joseph Hornblow and his wife Elsie produced Joseph and Harriet Smallcombe's first great-grandchild, Douglas Frederick. Then there were the marriages of two more grandchildren, those of Joseph and Harriet's first granddaughter Gladys Constance Hornblow, daughter of Harriet Hannah; and Ernest Douglas Smallcombe Weeks the son of Rhoda Rose.

The first marriage on Monday the 21st of June 1920, was that of Gladys, aged twenty five, who gave her address as the Bridge Hotel, Bute Street, Cardiff, when she married Christopher John Pratt, aged twenty six, a Printer's Chief Clerk, of North Road, Gabalfa, Cardiff.

Gladys's father, the late William Hornblow, was recorded as a Licensed Victualler (Retired) (Deceased), and Christopher's father Alfred Pratt gave his occupation as a coal trimmer (retired). The witnesses at the United Methodist Church in Miskin Street were D. Evan Jones, and L.M. Travers. Gladys' address at the Bridge Hotel is quite significant, because it proves that Harriet Hannah, a widow of some four years, had taken over the Bridge Hotel from a William C. Thomas, who was recorded as the proprietor in 1919, some time before June 21st 1920. She was to remain there for the rest of her life.

The marriage of Ernest Weeks, the first of Rhoda's children to marry, took place at the Cardiff Register Office on Monday the 22nd of November 1920; three weeks after Joseph celebrated his seventieth birthday. Ernest, aged twenty seven, of 77 Wyndham Street, Cardiff, was recorded as a carpenter, and his father Samuel Ernest Venning Weeks was recorded as a Baker and Confectioner. Ernest's bride was the twenty four year old Hilda Minnie Davies of 18 Gordon Road, Cardiff. Her father, the late Job Davies was recorded as being 'of independent means', and the witnesses to the marriage were Ernest's father Samuel, and an E. M Hull. The family name of Hull is not known, other that at the time that Joseph and Harriet were at the Westgate Hotel there was a Hull family in the High Street at the Bluebell Inn.

At the end of 1921, Ernest Douglas Weeks and his wife Hilda Minnie then gave Joseph and Harriet a second great-grandson, Douglas Ernest Davies Weeks.

It would appear on the surface that 1920 and 1921 were years of celebration for Joseph and his family, but as any parent will testify it is not possible to divorce oneself from the problems of one's children, even if the children are middle aged or beyond. In this respect Joseph must have been troubled by the problems being created in the Hornblow household by his daughter's drinking. It was known by Harriet Hannah's sister Beatrice in Yate that Harriet Hannah had pledged to drink herself to death, although probably the threat was not taken seriously.

It has been established that by 1920 Joseph's daughter, the widow Harriet Hannah Hornblow, had become the licensee of the Bridge Hotel, and living with her was her daughter Gladys Constance, her husband Christopher Pratt, Harriet Hannah's son Frederick Joseph, and his wife Elsie. It is said that one day Harriet Hannah came downstairs at the Bridge Hotel, and found her daughter Gladys Constance and husband Chris, together with Frederick Joseph and his wife Elsie, laughing and joking at the foot of the stairs. Possibly Harriet Hannah overheard something at which she took offence, but for whatever reason she ordered the children out of the hotel. As Frederick Joseph's son Douglas was only a babe in arms at the time, this would date the incident around early spring 1920, at which time Frederick Joseph was the manager of the Splott Cinema, and the Clifton Cinema just around the corner. It is even stated in local records that Frederick Joseph was known as a kindly manager who always wore a bowler hat and 'tails', which conjures up an amusing picture when combined with the family anecdote of Frederick Joseph cycling between cinemas with reels of film.

Following the incident at the Bridge Hotel Frederick Joseph and Elsie found accommodation in a back room in Pomeroy Street, Docks, with very primitive facilities, but shortly afterwards moved in with Elsie's mother, whilst Gladys Constance and her husband Chris Pratt moved to Landsdown Road. It was Elsie's mother, Elizabeth Griffiths, who took baby Douglas to see Harriet Hannah and caused a reconciliation, as might be confirmed by the photograph of Harriet Hannah with grandson Douglas aged between twelve and eighteen months, this must have been taken about the summer of 1921.

Harriet Hannah & Douglas

It is probable that at about this time Frederick Joseph Hornblow and his wife Elsie took over Harriet Hannah's house at 242 Cathedral Road. Harriet Hannah had not been shown to be there since 1918, and Frederick and Elsie were shown to be living there by the time the 1924 Directory was published.

This, however, is not the end of the saga as there is now a contribution from the Yate side of the family. It appears that Harriet Hannah's sister Beatrice sent her daughter Sarah from Yate to the Bridge Hotel in Cardiff, as Harriet Hannah was unwell. It is said that Sarah was seventeen at the time, and this ties in with the known facts, as by the spring of 1920 Sarah would have been seventeen, and it looks as if Sarah was sent to cover for the evicted family. The Yate version of the story says that Harriet Hannah's son, Frederick Joseph, being twenty-three, took exception to Sarah being in charge of the Bridge Hotel as he considered himself to be senior to Sarah, but Sarah being a somewhat ebullient character stuck to her guns. Now, Frederick Joseph would have been twenty three in August 1921, and at that time Sarah would have been eighteen, so again we have a remarkably good consensus on dates, particularly bearing in mind the acceptable discrepancies in family stories passed down through several generations. It appears that Sarah stayed at the Bridge Hotel until the spring of 1923, having been in Cardiff for up to three years, before returning to live at the School House in North Road, Yate, and then to work at the pin mill at Charfield, about five miles from Yate. Although it is not strictly part of the Joseph story it is worth recording that the pin mill, apart from almost certainly making metal pins, manufactured sewing and knitting needles from animal bone, and it is said that a quantity of bone meal found its way from time to time into the bean rows in Yate.

There is no record of Joseph being involved in the problems surrounding Harriet Hannah in the spring or summer of 1921, but it is unlikely that he was unaware or unaffected by the situation. Unfortunately tragedy was, yet again, not too far behind, when within six months of the birth of Douglas Ernest Davies Weeks, Joseph and Harriet suffered the death of their only other son, William Albert Jones Smallcombe. He died of bronchitis on Tuesday the 4th April 1922 aged forty; he too died at home at 12 Allerton Street. Like his brother he was unmarried, and did not leave a will, but he was referred to as a master haulier by trade, although he does not appear in any directories as such.

William was the fifth of Joseph and Harriet's eight children to pre-decease them. Joseph, who was at his son's bedside when he died, recorded the death at the West Cardiff Register Office on the same day that his son died. The grave L183 at Cathays cemetery was filled when the burial of Frederick Joseph had taken place, so Joseph purchased another plot in the extension of Cathays Cemetery at Allensbank Road, plot EI 1439. It was here that William Albert was buried, and where in the fullness of time Joseph and Harriet were to be laid to rest. None of the family graves has a headstone.

Even the death of William did not finish the predeceasing of Joseph and Harriet by their children. Their widowed daughter Harriet Hannah Hornblow, of the Bridge Hotel, Bute Street, Cardiff, who although not yet fifty years of age, but recorded as being fifty-one, died on Thursday the 8th of February 1923, of cirrhosis of the liver and heart failure. Harriet Hannah had been a widow for eight years, and her son Frederick Joseph, now a barman, was with her when she died, and it was he who registered the death the following day. There is a strong possibility that Frederick Joseph was a barman at the Bridge Hotel, helping Sarah during his mother's last illness.

At her death Harriet was still the proprietor of the Bridge Hotel, Bute Street, although her son Frederick lived at 242 Cathedral Road. On Monday the 12th February, Harriet Hannah was laid to rest with her husband at Cathays Cemetery, in grave V225. Once more the undertaker was Mr. A. J. Stone, and by now the cost of the interment had risen considerably to two pounds fourteen-shillings and sixpence, fifteen-shillings being the interment, and one pound nineteen-and-sixpence for the digging; the Vicar received ten-shillings.

As it is part of the family story as related down the generations it should be recorded that, on her return to Yate, Sarah confided to the family that she was unhappy with the way Harriet Hannah died. She said that a 'foreign' doctor called to see Harriet Hannah, and gave her an injection, and she never regained consciousness. The doctor who signed the death certificate was R. C. Shepherd MB., which does not seem particularly 'foreign', and although what Sarah said might be true, it would not necessarily imply anything sinister.

One wonders if Joseph and Harriet felt some particular remorse over the death of their daughter. Harriet had been a barmaid since she was a teenager, living in public houses surrounded by families of Licensed Victuallers, and the manner of her death indicates a addiction to alcohol. Harriet Hannah left a will, which she made on the 23rd of August 1921, leaving her entire estate, of one thousand seven-hundred and twenty-one pounds, five-shillings and sixpence gross, one thousand four-hundred and eighty-five pounds, sixteen-shillings and nine-pence net, to her "youngest son Frederick Joseph Hornblow of 242 Cathedral Road". Frederick was the sole executor, and the witnesses were her solicitor, Barnett Janner, and his clerk, Doris L. Dowling. Probate was granted on the 11th May 1923. Nothing was left to her daughter Gladys, and nothing to her son William Lionel.

We can be sure that there was a continuing family bond between the Hornblow side of the family and Joseph and Harriet, as it is known in family circles that Frederick Joseph continued to visit his grandparents at 12 Allerton Street after the death of his parents.

What a mixed year this was for the Smallcombe family, for 1923 saw yet another two great-grandchildren for Joseph and Harriet. On the 24th of June, at 170 Whitchurch Road, Gabalfa, Cardiff, Gladys and Christopher Pratt had a son Norman Christopher, and shortly afterwards moved to Longspears Avenue. Later in the summer, on July 18th Frederick and Elsie Hornblow had a son, Frederick John, the third and fourth great-grandsons for Joseph and Harriet.

By the beginning of 1924 Joseph was just turned seventy-four years of age, and in some Directories of 1921-24 he is still listed as a resident at 12 Allerton Street, and he is still referred to as a haulier, although he still does not have an entry in the business section. It is unlikely that Joseph continued the haulage business on his own account or even 'fronted' the business for a grandson or other relative, as there are none without a continuous occupation, or in a suitable position to take over the business.

In the Spring of 1926, William G. Hornblow, born to Frederick and Elsie was the fifth, and last, great-grandson to be born during Joseph's lifetime, and in that year on the 27th July 1926, now aged seventy-six, he made out his will in which he describes himself as "A Gentleman". This is compatible with the fact that the Directories from 1924 to 1927 list Joseph as living at 12 Allerton Street, with no occupation.

At this time Joseph and Harriet lived just over a quarter of a mile from Ninian Park, the home of Cardiff City F.C., so they could hardly have been unaware of the excitement that year when Cardiff City became the first football club to take the F.A. Cup out of England, by beating Arsenal at Wembley on the 23rd of April 1927. If Joseph had been a Cardiff City supporter he would only have had to walk down Allerton Street, turn right into Cornwall Street, pass under the railway bridge, into Virgil Street, and turn right up Sloper Road to the ground, a five minute walk.

In his seventy- seventh year Joseph faced yet another family death. On Thursday the 19th of May 1927 his son-in-law, Samuel Ernest Venning Weeks the husband of his daughter Rose Rhoda, died of prostate cancer and kidney failure. Samuel was only fifty-nine years of age, and was described as a 'hospital baker'. He died at 77 Wyndham Street, West Cardiff, with his son Ernest Douglas, of 126 Brunswick Street, Cardiff, at his bedside.

Happily the last family event, a few months before Joseph died, was the birth of a great granddaughter Rita Hornblow. This was the last of Frederick Joseph and Elise's children, but Joseph and Harriet's first great granddaughter.

Ninian Park in the 1930s

85

# Chapter Nine

## The End of Joseph's Story
### 31st December 1931

Joseph as a young boy had a very hard start to life, and as a mature man it was an ever flowing mixture of joy and grief, perhaps more grief than the average family man had to suffer even in those Victorian days, but it has to be said that even Joseph's death had an element of pathos about it. On 7th December 1931, Joseph, aged eighty one died at 12 Allerton Street, Grangetown, Cardiff, of complications following an accident when one of the large double doors between 12 and 10 Allerton Street, which formed the entrance to the yard, and which had been taken off ready for painting, fell on him.

His death certificate reads,

"Cause of Death. Hypostatic pneumonia and chronic bronchitis accelerated through being confined to bed following injuries to hips and sides sustained through a garage door accidentally falling upon him. No P.M."

The local paper carried a notice in the Deaths section,

"Smallcombe.- December 7th, at 12 Allerton-street, Joseph, the beloved husband of Harriet Smallcombe. Funeral Saturday 11am., for Cardiff Cemetery."

Even then there is still a twist in the tale. Joseph is recorded in the Western Mail Directory as a haulier from 1927 to 1932. The 1932 Directory would have been composed before Joseph died but nevertheless he was eighty-one at the time. One can only assume that for some years the Directories had not updated their information, perhaps relying on contributors to cancel out of date entries.

In spite of the directories his Death Certificate, on which the Informant is shown as "Certificate received from Gerald Tudor Coroner for Cardiff inquest held 9th December 1931", shows that he was "An old age Pensioner (formerly a pickle merchant)". It appears that perhaps Joseph's last occupation was indeed the pickle business.

86

# Post Mortem

So, in the final analysis what did Joseph leave behind him? In his will proved on the 16th January 1932 at Llandaff, he left seven hundred and seventy-three pounds, sixteen-shillings and seven-pence gross; three hundred and twenty-nine pounds, sixteen-shillings and nine-pence net. Everything was left to his wife Harriet, and she was granted probate, with John Lewis, on the 16th January 1932. This figure is commensurate with that left later by Harriet, but is less than half the sum left by their daughter Harriet Hannah Hornblow some ten years earlier. It is not possible to compare the sum of seven hundred and seventy-three pounds in 1932 with an exact amount in the year 2001, but that sum would have bought two or three terraced houses similar to the ones in which Joseph lived, which today might cost in the region of sixty-five thousand pounds each. In fact on 14th March 1919 there was a sale of leasehold dwellings and numbers 53, 55, 57, and 59 Kent Street were sold for seven hundred and ninety pounds as one lot, number 61 sold for two hundred pounds, and numbers 1 and 2 Little Dock Street sold for two hundred and sixty-five pounds the pair. So in those terms Joseph's estate would have been about one hundred and fifty to two hundred thousand pounds, but house prices have risen much faster than the value of money in any other sector, so this is too high a value. A labourer's wages around that period would have been about one pound ten-shillings per week, the modern equivalent would probably be about two hundred pounds, and on this basis Joseph's estate would have had an equivalent value of one hundred thousand pounds. One of the many overall comparative tables from numerous reference books shows the value of seven hundred and seventy-three pounds in the 1930s to be equivalent of thirty-five thousand pounds in the year 2001, and this reflects the lower cost, pro rata, of many commodities, due to more efficient production and better preservative methods for food etc. All we can really say is that Joseph's estate was what one might have expected from a reasonably well off retired middle class pensioner.

More importantly Joseph left a family, his wife Harriet now eighty-two, and two daughters, Rhoda Rose, aged fifty-six, and Beatrice, aged fifty-two. At his death he also had nine grandchildren, Gladys Constance, thirty-seven, William Lionel, thirty-eight, and

Frederick Joseph Hornblow, thirty-three; Ernest Douglas, thirty-eight, Daisy Constance, thirty-six, and Dorothy May Weeks, thirty four; Beatrice Williamina thirty-one, Harriet Sarah, twenty-nine, and Henry George Washbourne, twenty-four. He also had seven great-grandchildren, Norman Christopher Pratt, eight; Douglas Frederick, eleven, Frederick John, eight, William G., five, and Rita Hornblow, six months; and finally Douglas Ernest Weeks aged ten.

There is, however, an interesting anomaly in the comparative life spans of the members of Joseph's family. A study of the deaths of the elderly by Mary Pearce in 1997 showed that between 1837 and 1900 if a child survived to the age of ten years, it was more likely to die over the age of sixty, than at any age between ten and sixty. The study showed an increasing life expectancy, which indicates that children were likely to outlive their parents, and die at a greater age than their parents. Joseph's family were perverse in all of these matters. It will be recalled that Joseph died aged eighty-one, somewhat prematurely, as a result of an accident, and his wife Harriet died aged eight-four. In both cases bronchitis was a factor, and in the case of Harriet, heart failure. Only two of Joseph and Harriet's eight children outlived their parents, and only one of the eight children lived beyond sixty years. In fact none of the remainder got within twenty years of the age attained by their parents. Two of the children died before reaching the age of five, one died aged nineteen, three died in their forties, one at sixty, and one at ninety - three. The causes of the deaths of the children are more understandable, two died of tuberculosis, one of catarrh, one of bronchitis, one of bronchitis and heart failure, one of heart failure and senility, one of measles and one of cirrhosis. It is notable that of the ten members of the family seven died with ailments of the chest and lungs as a contributory factor.

There is nobody known to be alive today who knew Joseph, and few anecdotes as to his character, other than that he was a careful man in money matters, but he was clearly a man who influenced his family a great deal. Joseph was at various times a labourer, cabbie, barman, licensee, licensed victualler, and a wine and spirit merchant. His three daughters were at some time barmaids for Joseph. One son-in-law at his marriage to Joseph's daughter was a hydraulic attendant, his father being a contractor, with no apparent connections with the licence trade. This son-in-law became a barman, a licensed victualler, a spirits vault cellar man, and a taxicab proprietor; his death certificate showed him as a retired licensed victualler. Although Joseph's second son-in-law remained in his trade as a baker, Joseph's third son-in-law, who was a farmer as was his father before him, also became a licensee.

Shortly after Joseph's death his wife Harriet left Cardiff, and moved back to her roots, which happily for her was by coincidence where her daughter Beatrice now lived. Beatrice, now fifty-two years old, and her husband Harry Washbourne kept the Codrington Arms in North Road, Yate. Certainly Harriet was in Yate by the 18th July 1932 when she made her will.

The fact that Harriet moved away from the bulk of her family in Cardiff to the home of Beatrice in Yate might mean nothing other than that she wanted to get back to her roots. Having said that, Harriet, who had lived with Joseph in Cardiff for sixty years, must have had many friends as well as family, although she had quite possibly outlived many of them. The terms of her will, however, indicate that there might have been some division in the family.

Harriet died at the Codrington Arms on the 4th May 1934 aged eighty-four, of bronchitis and influenza. On her death certificate she is recorded as the widow of Joseph, a mineral water manufacturer, not a pickle merchant. In her will Harriet left six hundred and forty-eight pounds, fifteen-shillings and three-pence gross; three hundred and seventy-seven pounds, seventeen-shillings and nine-pence net. Rhoda Weeks, her daughter of 77 Wyndham Street, Riverside, Cardiff, was left fifty pounds, and Beatrice was left a leasehold house, 16 Clare Road, and the remainder of the estate of more than three hundred pounds. The address of 16 Clare Road has not been noted before, but from 1930 to 1933 was occupied by Albert Patterson and his family, with Philip and Emma Gibbs. Clearly Beatrice was favoured above Harriet's only other surviving child Rhoda. Nothing was left to the Hornblow family, although in fairness to Harriet she had no surviving children within that family, and Harriet had not left anything in her will other than to her children. Probate was granted to Beatrice on the 22nd June 1934, and at her specific request Harriet was interred in Cardiff with her late husband

Joseph, and her son William Albert, in the Cathays Cemetery, plot E1, 1439.

16 Clare Road

So how did the family fare after Joseph's death? Clearly the Smallcombe name was to die out in this branch of the family when William Albert died without issue in 1922. As we have seen, only two of the children survived Joseph and Harriet, Rhoda Rose, described by a grandchild as a being a smart stern lady, who died in 1968 aged ninety-three, and Beatrice, who died in 1940, aged sixty.

Harriet Hannah Smallcombe's descendents still survive in the Hornblow and Pearce families. Rhoda Rose Smallcombe's descendents still survive in the family of Douglas Ernest Weeks, which included Dorothy May Weeks who died in 1999 aged a hundred and two, and Beatrice Smallcombe's family still survives in the Hollister family in Yate.

# APPENDIX

| Joseph-Harriet Date Line | Occupations - Home & World Events |
|---|---|
| 1849 Harriet Dyer, b. Iron Acton | Invention of the safety pin |
| 1850 Joseph - b. workhouse Yate | San Francisco gold rush |
| 1851 Joseph - at Yate workhouse | First breach loaded rifle |
| 1852-9 No records | Crimean War 1853 - 56 |
| 1860 Joseph 10 years old | Professional education in nursing |
| 1861 Joseph - workhouse Yate | **Farm servant.** American Civil War 1861-65 |
| 1862-9 No records | 1864 Clifton Suspension Bridge open |
| 1870 Joseph 20 years old | Stanley & Livingston meet in Congo |
| 1871 Both at White Hart, Bristol | **Ostler/maid.** Formation of German Empire |
| 1872 Married - Lamb St., Bristol | **Brewer.** Albert Memorial completed |
| 1873 11 Eclipse St. Bristol | **Labourer.** Daughter Harriet Hannah born |
| 1874 No record | Penny farthing bicycle comes into use |
| 1875 9 Eclipse St., Cardiff | **Labourer.** Daughter Rhoda Rose born |
| 1876 93 Clifton St., Cardiff | G. A. Bell patents the telephone |
| 1877 93 Clifton St., Cardiff | **Cab driver.** Sound recorded by T. Edison |
| 1877 73 Elm St., Cardiff | Son Frederick Joseph born |
| 1877 13 Lily St., Cardiff | Internal combustion engine invented |
| 1878 65 Sandon Terrace | First telephone switchboard opened |
| 1879 65 Sandon Terrace** | **Barman.** Two stroke auto engine produced |
| 1879 65 Adam Street ** | Daughter Beatrice born |
| 1880 65 Adam Street | Modern form of bicycle developed |
| 1881 65 Adam Street | **Barman -** son William Albert Jones born |
| 1882 65 Adam Street | Jesse James killed by own gang member |
| 1883 88 Adam Street | **Club manager -** dter Florence Blanche born |
| 1884 88 Adam Street | **Barman -** dter Alice Maud Mary born |
| 1885 Westgate Hotel | **Licensee -** dter Lily Ada born |
| 1886 Westgate Hotel | **Hotel Keeper/Publican -** dter Lily Ada died |
| 1887 Westgate Hotel | **Licensee -** gramophone invented |
| 1888 Westgate Hotel | **Licensee -** dter Alice Maud Mary died |
| 1889 Westgate Hotel | **Licensee -** Eiffel Tower built |
| 1889 38 Clare Rd./Allerton St. | **Min. water manuf.-** First steam turbine |
| 1890 Westgate Hotel | **Lic.victualler (1891)** - synth. rubber produced |

| Joseph-Harriet Date Line | Occupations - Home & World Events |
|---|---|
| 1891 Westgate Hotel | **Wine-sp.Merch.**- dter Harriet Hannah marr. |
| 1892 (46 Clare Road?) | **Wine-spMerch** – dter Rhoda Rose marr. |
| 1892 | Granddter Harriet Hornblow born |
| 1893 32 Clare Road | **Wine-Sp.Merchant** |
| 1893 | Grdsons W.L.Hornblow/E.D.S. Weeks born |
| 1894 32 Clare Rd./Allerton St. | Granddter Gladys C. Hornblow born |
| 1894 67 Clare Road | First motion pictures |
| 1895 36, 67 Clare Rd./Allerton St. | Granddter Daisy C. Weeks born |
| 1896 36, 67 Clare Rd./Allerton St. | Klondike gold rush |
| 1897 38 Clare Road | Granddter Dorothy May Weeks born |
| 1897 67 Clare Rd/14 Allerton St. | Queen Victoria Diamond Jubilee |
| 1898 38 Clare Road | Grandson Frederick J. Hornblow born |
| 1899 38 Clare Road | Relief of Ladysmith, Boer War 1899-1902 |
| 1900 38 Clare Rd./Allerton St. | **Min. water manuf**. - dter Beatrice married |
| 1900 | Granddter Williamina Washbourne born |
| 1901 38 Clare Rd./Allerton St. | Queen Victoria died |
| 1902 12 Allerton St./38 Clare Rd. | **Min.wter manuf**-dtr Florence Blanche died |
| 1902 | Granddter Harriet S. Washbourne born |
| 1903-5 12 Allerton St./38 Clare Rd. | 1903 Wright Bros. first air machine |
| 1906 12 Allerton St./38 Clare Rd. | **Min. water manuf**. First telegraphic picture |
| 1907 12 Allerton St./38 Clare Rd. | Grandson Henry G. Washbourne born |
| 1908-9 12 Allerton St./38 Clare Rd. | 1908 Introduction of O. A. Pension (70+) |
| 1910 12 Allerton St./38 Clare Rd. | Joseph aged 60 - Edward VII died |
| 1911-4 12 Allerton St./38 Clare Rd. | Shop workers max. 60 hour week. |
| 1915 12 Allerton Street | Joseph aged 65 - William Hornblow died |
| 1916 12 Allerton Street | First tank used in warfare |
| 1917 No record | Grandson Frederick J. Hornblow married |
| 1918 12 Allerton Street | **Haulier** - son Frederick Joseph died |
| 1918 | Grandson William L. Hornblow married |
| 1919 12 Allerton Street | First atom split & first woman M.P. |
| 1920 12 Allerton Street | **Haulier**(70)-grnddtr Gladys Hornblow marr. |
| 1920 | Grandson Ernest D. S. Weeks married |
| 1920 | G-Grandson Douglas F. Hornblow born |
| 1921 12 Allerton Street | **Haulier**. G-grndsn D.E. D. Weeks born |

| Joseph-Harriet Date Line | Occupations - Home & World Events |
|---|---|
| 1922  12 Allerton Street | **Haulier** - son William Albert Jones died |
| 1923  No records | **Haulier** - daughter Harriet Hannah died |
| 1923 | G-Grandson Norman C. Pratt born |
| 1923 | G-Grandson Frederick J. Hornblow born |
| 1924  12 Allerton Street | **Haulier.**C24etrol 1/8d p.gal.- under 2p.litre |
| 1925  12 Allerton Street | Teacher fined (US) for teaching evolution |
| 1926  12 Allerton Street | **Gentleman.** G-Grdsn W.G.Hornblow born |
| 1927  12 Allerton Street | **Haulier.** S. Ernest V. Weeks died |
| 1928-9 12 Allerton Street | **Haulier.** 1928 Penicillin discovered |
| 1930  12 Allerton Street | **Haulier** - aged 80. Nylon invented |
| 1931  12 Allerton Street | Joseph died. G-Grnddtr Rita Hornblow born |
| 1932  *12 Allerton Street* | ***Haulier.*** Grnddter Harriet Washbourne marr. |
| 1932  Harriet at Codrington Arms | Nurses not to work over 13 hrs a day |
| 1933  Harriet at Codrington Arms | Grandson Henry G. Washbourne married |
| 1934  Harriet at Codrington Arms | 1934 Harriet died |

```
****************************************************************
****************************************************************
```

## Currency and Measurements

For those not familiar with pre-decimal currency, a pound was divided into 240 pence; with 12 pence (12d) to a shilling (1/-); and 20 shillings (20/-) to a pound (£).

| Decimal currency | Old money | (designation/colloquially) |
|---|---|---|
| £1.00 | £1.0.0. | (a pound/quid) |
| 75p | 15/- | (fifteen shillings/ fifteen bob) |
| 50p | 10/- | (ten shillings/ten bob/half a knicker} |
| 25p | 5/- | (five shillings/five bob/dollar) |
| 12.5p | 2/6d | (two and six[pence]/half a crown) |
| 10p | 2/- | (florin/ two bob)) |
| 5p | 1/- | (a shilling/a bob) |
| 2.5 p | 6d | (sixpence/tanner) |
| 1.25p | 3d | (three pence, pronounced "thrupence" or thre'pence") |

The silver "thrupenny bit was called a "joey"). Two pennies would be termed "tuppence". 1d (penny/copper) was divided into two halfpennies (ha'pennies), or four farthings.

There were also a number of peculiar usages, such as cloth, which was sold by the yard. As in present times an item valued at £1 is usually sold at 99p, so cloth would be sold at 'four-eleven-three', which translates as four-shillings and eleven pence three farthings, instead of five-shillings.

93

# BIBLIOGRAPHY

Most of the information in the text is taken from birth, death and marriage certificates, from the Register Offices in Cardiff and Yate; military records, and wills from the Public Records Offices and the Commonwealth Graves Commission; local directories, old street maps, censuses, and burial records, from Newport and Cardiff Libraries and Archives; and workhouse records from the Gloucestershire Record Office. The co-operation and efforts of all these repositories is much appreciated.

I also acknowledge the value of several specialist books, namely:

The Cardiff Yesterday Series - Stewart Williams.
Coal Metropolis Cardiff 1870–1914, M.J. Daunton, Leicester University Press-1977.
Occupational Costume in England, Cunningham & Lucas, A. & C. Black, 1976.
History of Everyday things in England 1851-1914, M&C Quinnell, Batsford 1952.
The Illustrated History of the Housewife, Una Robertson, Sutton, 1999
The Rise and Fall of the Victorian Servant, Pamela Horn, Sutton, 1995
The History of the London Horse Cab, Trevor May, Alan Sutton Publishing, 1995
Local Historian's Encyclopaedia, John Richardson, Historical Publications, 1974
A Study of the Care and Provision for Elderly People from an Historical
                              Perspective, unpublished 1997, by Mary H. Pearce.

**Directories:** Kellys (various),  Slaters, Cardiff & District Trade, Wrights, Butchers Post Office, Cardiff Western Mail, Websters, Scammell & Co., Hunt & Co., Bristol & County,  and Pigots.
*
There is an invaluable internet site, "The Victorian Web"

## Index of Characters

Any person with more than 10 entries is show "From page .."

## Index of Characters Non Family

## Index of places outside Cardiff

# Index of places in Cardiff

**General Interest**

Agricultural Labourer:-62

Air (frame) Mechanic:-75,77,78

Aircraft, RAF, RFC,RNAS:-71,77,78

Armourer:-78

Baker-Master:-44,46,47,73,80,85,89

Barmaid:-40,88,

Barman:-22,23,25,26,27,43,44,46,83

Blacksmith:-11,13,14,40,66

Boer War:-47,63

Bowler and Top hats:-37

Breeches, gaiters, leggings, smock:-6

Brewer:-9,10

Buses and trams:-17,18,64,67,71

Cab Fares:-70

Cab hire/purchase/costs:-17,20,21,22

Cab ranks:-18

Candles, Gas, Electric light:-29, 30

Carts and traps:-71,72,74

Charwoman:-23,34

Cholera:-4

Coal :-10,11,30,62,80

Cod's wallop and twaddle:-50

Cordial Manufacturer:-42

Dock labourer:-23   Dock Master:-32

Drinking Clubs:-26

Electoral Roll (qualification):-19

Empire Day:-63

Engine Driver, Engineer:-62,75,77

Farm Servant:-5 ::Farmer:-61,63,67

Farrier, Carriages, Wheelwright:-66

Film Printer:-78

Fire & House/Friendly Soc. Agent:-23

Great War (Germany):-71,74-77,79

Hansom Cab:-16,17,18,19-21,,69

Haulier/haulage:55,65,74,79,83,84,86

Horses:-7,10,17,19,21,55,69,70,71

Hospital:-32

Hydraulic Attendant:-41

Internal combustion engine:-17

Labourer:-14,20,23

Licensed Trade:- from page 40

Luxury goods:-45,49

Machinery & ingredients:-49 to 63

Married Women's Property Act:-40

Medical:-71,72,76,79,82,83,85,86,88,89

Military, Militia:-17,26,71

Mineral Water Manuf.:-from page37

Mines & Collieries Act 1842:-10

Mortgage:-68

Motor Cycle Taxi:-70

Motor driver:-74,77

Music Halls:-45

Nurse - Head Nurse:-34,35

Petrol:-70

Pickle Manufacturer:-50,73,74,86,89

Pin Mill, pins & needles:-82

Printer's Chief Clerk:-79

Privy, Earth Closet, W.C.:-6

Railway:-17,42,68,85

Rents:-14

Rubber tyres:-17

Scattered houses:-32

Taxi:-17,18,19,68,69,70:-meter 17

Telephone/telegraph:-17

Vaccination:-4

Votes for Women:-79

Wages:-3,8,14,19-21,24,49,87

Welsh Sunday Closing Act 1881:26

Workhouse Master:-5